# Wild Women Write.
## RE-CONNECTING WITH THE WILD FEMININE

# by Marjorie St. Clair

ISBN: 9781080022953

Earth Muse Press
2000 Aina Mahi'ai St.
Lahaina, Maui, 96761

# ACKNOWLEDGMENTS

Much of the material in this book including the writing exercises were gleaned from experiences and feedback from the many incredible wild women who have taken writing classes from me over the years, specifically those who took the series called *Wild Women Write*. These remarkable women have inspired me with their willingness to dive into their deep psyches to explore the Wild Woman archetype and to write about their experience and insights. In one of the first *Wild Women Write* series, nothing was off limits, an attitude that led to a performance piece called *Yoni Speaks* where women read their writing to an appreciative audience, also inspired by their braveness in telling their deepest and often traumatic stories regarding their sexuality and sexual experiences. The willingness of the women in the *Wild Women Write* classes to become fully aware of their untamed emotions and instinctual natures and to take responsibility for how to express them with conscious awareness inspired me to take on the task of charting the Wild Woman journey inside a book that insisted that I, too, listen and heed the Call of the Wild Woman.

And to those many women through the ages who have risen above their daily lives of whatever description to put their words and thoughts to stone, clay, page and screen—Thank You. Your collective voices have informed and carried us all forward in our efforts to better educate ourselves and to become more aware of our "arrow of time" in the history of human beings, especially as women.

Special thanks to graphic designer, artist & muralist Denise Weaver Ross, whose amazing skills and knowledge helped me get the book into a beautiful format and for her assistance in helping me to navigate the many steps required to publish. Her unique and recognizable artistic talent also created the original artwork for the book cover of *Wild Women Write*.

Finally, an acknowledgment and deepest gratitude to my daughter Suzanne Canja who has been my constant ally encouraging me in all my crazy-wild-and sometimes magnificent endeavors throughout this life. And to the many wonderful wild women and men who have peopled my life and supported me in ways equally mad and inspiring! Of course, hugs and kisses to all the plants, animals and spirit allies who have propped me up and given me the courage to continue on when, as my favorite poet Mary Oliver says, "Meanwhile the wild geese, high in the clean blue air, are heading home again. Whoever you are, no matter how lonely, the world offers itself to your imagination, calls to you like the wild geese, harsh and exciting—over and over announcing your place in the family of things."

# TABLE OF CONTENTS

# Wild Women Write:
## RE-CONNECTING WITH THE WILD FEMININE

## by Marjorie St. Clair

# INTRODUCTION

In ancient times, so we are told, the call of the wilderness was considered a call from spirit. Those who dwelt in the forest places were said to be living in the "in between places" of the Otherworld and the Ordinary world in order to learn how to merge or become one with all of nature. Myths say that these forest dwellers grew feathers on their bodies like the birds. Some say they could fly like the birds; still others of a more doubtful nature wondered if they were simply wearing feathered cloaks that made them look like strange birds when seen between the branches of a tree. Other forest dwellers were said to run with the herds of wild deer and live on wild plants like the deer themselves, reminiscent of the stories of the Greek Goddess Artemis, Lady of the Wild Things, who roamed the forest places with her animals and bare-breasted nymphs.

But what about women today for whom that close connection to the wild things and their own instinctual natures may have gone missing in their lives? What about women who have so superficially tamed their wild instinctual natures represented by the Wild Woman archetype that in the process they have cut themselves off from the very wellsprings of their own creative source. D. H. Lawrence called this "bleeding at the roots."

If one assumes that we've lost our connections to our instinctual roots, as I do, then where can we look to reclaim and experience that aspect of ourselves that is embedded in the Wild Woman archetype? *Wild Women Write* was born out of my own journey of discovery in searching for the wild woman and subsequent efforts in helping other women in their search for a deeper connection to their wildish essence.

Through the years of searching and re-connecting with that mysterious something inside myself that I experienced as my core essence, I joined with other like-minded women and men in celebrating the earth and our joy at being alive and able to contribute to the global dream of making the world a better place for ourselves and our children after us. Gradually, as I aged and became an elder I began to teach and lead women on vision quests into the desert to re-connect with their own inner powerful wild woman. While living on Maui during the 1980s and 90s, I joined with a group of other women, calling ourselves *WomanSpirit*. We came together to mark the cycles of the seasons and of women's blood mysteries with ritual and ceremony. We did this because we felt it was important. We felt it mattered. We felt it was a way to care for our souls and revive the dying spirits of nature. We felt it was a way for us to re-connect wirh our instinctual natures, our wildwoman selves. We were smart enough to recognize that while we had been busy tending to how our outside looked, we had lost touch with our inner self.

Through our rituals and support of one another, we grew ourselves into magical women by turning to nature to heal us. In nature we were able to reclaim those lost parts of our psyches, our dark and powerful instinctual natures that had lain buried for thousands of lifetimes. We painted ancient symbols on our bodies and cavorted naked under the full moon, singing and dancing and drumming into the wee hours of the night. Clarissa Estes-Pinkola told us in her inspiring book *Women Who Run With Wolves* that the wild woman was an endangered species. One of the ways to keep our wolf nature alive, our wild woman alive, so she said, was to regularly howl at the moon.

And so we did! We sought out the wild places on the island where the spirits of place were still palpable and alive with all the magical energies of Hawaii. It was Pele the Goddess of volcanoes who had called most of us to the islands from her fiery depths, promising renewal on land forged from the fire in Her belly. We answered Her call and showed up, and we grew, and grew and grew and are still growing.

When the spirit of the southwestern desert places called me to return, I did. As I searched for an appropriate way to share what I considered to be of great importance in evolving our western culture's myths to include an equality of all and featuring the earth as the main character in a new narrative, I knew that women's voices weren't being heard in the numbers they deserved. I decided to devote myself to teaching writing, with a primary focus on women and their writing. The talented and creative women I've been privileged to work with over this last decade who rose to the challenge of finding their inner passion, wisdom and unique individual voices in their writing inspired me to develop a writing class series called *Wild Women Write,* which included myths and stories, both ancient and modern of strong and powerful heroines along with provocative writing exercises intended to give women the opportunity to share their written responses in a safe and supportive setting while exploring their lives in a deeper way. Over the last five years in the *Wild Women Write* classes, women have been courageously diving deep into their psyches and re-connecting with aspects of themselves they'd discarded, or feared and brought them back to their conscious awareness through their writing and sharing with one another. Self-discovery and empowerment have been some of their rewards, in addition to finding out what good writers they are with their own unique voices.

In order to release our instinctual feminine nature into a "creative and redemptive life," as author and Jungian analyst Marion Woodman has called it, we must actively seek out the Wild Woman, searching for her in her favorite haunts. In *Wild Women Write,* we look at myths and multiple other ways to find and reconnect with her archetype such as writing, sharing our insights on the material presented, and through personal and group art projects and ceremonies. We look to our dreams and our art where she speaks to us through symbols; or by looking for her where she has been hiding in plain sight inside myths or folk tales that we have dismissed as being for children only. Wild Woman still roams the wild places in nature and if we go there, listen quietly and with reverence, we will be able to feel her palpable presence. She is the heart of our creativity, sexuality and passion, which we give expression to through our rituals and in our relationships with one another. Once we have re-connected with her in meaningful ways, we have indeed released our instinctual feminine nature into a "creative and redemptive life."

This book is an offering to all women and the people who love them who are ready to explore and forge a connection with the fire in their bellies that emanates from their Wild Woman essence.

I've researched and included many stories and quite a bit of information that you may find less or more interesting or helpful. The same goes for the writing and art exercises generously sprinkled throughout the text. I encourage you to pick and choose what is relevant for you and to jump back and forth between chapters if that appeals to you. You may also want to gather a few friends together to read, write and share your writing and processes of self-discovery with one another.

Even if you don't consider yourself a writer, you can benefit from reading and reflecting on the myths and stories. Whatever your choice of using and interacting with the material, it will be a wild and wonderful ride. Listen intently to the Call of the Wild Woman and let her guide you in interacting with this book and in your life!

With love,
Marjorie Beene St.Clair

*Tutu Pele: Goddess of Volcanoes* by Siri Swenson
*Used with permission of the artist's heirs.*

# CHAPTER 1: Re-Connecting With the Wild Woman Archetype

*Put your ear down close to your soul*
*And listen hard*
~Anne Sexton

Who or what is the Wild Woman? What does it mean to remember this archetype and does it matter if we feel connected to it or not?

The Wild Woman is elusive, lives deep underground and is difficult to discover. Clarissa Pinkola-Estes, author of *Women Who Run with the Wolves*, has called her an endangered species that had to become invisible because her survival depended on it. During a period of time lasting well over two thousand years, it gradually became increasingly dangerous for women to fully express their wildish natures, to enjoy their sexuality, to sing songs and make poems exalting their yonis, to run with the wild animals, to dance and drum to ecstatic rituals intended to teach them how to be one with themselves and every other creature. Women of today have become an almost unrecognizable species when compared to their early female ancestors who were considered magical and sacred because they could bleed monthly and not die and could give live birth to both sexes.

Through the centuries patriarchal cultures worldwide evolved values, religions and societal norms to make sure that a woman knew her place, made sure she learned how to make herself physically beautiful so she could attract a good husband who presumably would take care of her and any children she birthed because they, like herself, had become the property of and belonged to the male. She learned to embrace values that made sure she remained docile, sweet, demure and yielding to her overlord, the male. Under the male patriarchy that replaced the earliest human tribes who worshipped and gave homage to a Great Mother Goddess, women were killed, raped, tortured, hung, burned to death and forced into slavery. Over time, it wasn't okay for a woman to be all of herself anymore. It wasn't okay for her to think and speak her mind. It wasn't okay to be a self-empowered woman, someone who stood tall in her own truth and beingness, especially, her wildish self that demanded to be free.

Gone were the wild magical beings who lived in the forest with their animals and cavorted with other wild creatures like nymphs, fairies and unicorns; gone were the stories of the all-knowing Mother Goddesses like Inanna and Isis who brought culture, organization and civilized ways for people to live peacefully together in communities; gone were the crazy-mad wild women who followed Artemis or the God of Wine Dionysus to experience their uncensored wild passionate instinctual natures; gone were the *hierodules* or sacred prostitutes of ancient Greece and Rome who had the freedom to choose what they wanted to do with their bodies and their minds.

Through the centuries that saw the birth and domination by a patriarchy, women had become property; they had learned how to manipulate and "make nice" in order to survive. Women's wildish natures were sent away, declared dangerous and were banished, never to be seen again if women "knew what was good for them." Now women had to learn to be respectable with good manners befitting a proper lady, requiring they know how to speak, how to stand, and, as I and many women of the late 20th century were taught, how to sit. For goodness sake, we were warned, don't sit with your legs uncrossed when you're in mixed company, because someone might see "down there" and behold the mysterious dark and forbidden region so feared by the male patriarchy and seat of the powerful dark feminine... the vulva.

In fact, the Wild Woman has been gone for so long that we've almost totally forgotten about her and how important her archetype is in connecting us with our instinctual natures. She's more like a ghost, a dim memory of some long ago time when women ran free as the wind, sky-clad and naked, with their long, loose tresses blowing behind them.

But Wild Woman isn't dead! She just disappeared for a great long while; that is, until over time and little by little things began to happen that caused her to stir again, things like a book called *Women Who Run With the Wolves*; until a Broadway play like Ntozake Shange's *For Colored Girls Who Have Considered Suicide When the Rainbow Is Enuf*; until the black dancer Josephine Baker moved to Paris in the 1920s and became the dancing darling of the burlesque world; until Hildegard von Bingen ignored all the rules and wrote poetry, music and essays about her mystical experiences all within the walls of a 12th century Benedictine abbey; until the French maid Joan of Arc illegally adorned herself in male armor and went off to fight the English and restore the French monarchy; or, as contemporary French feminist Monique Wittig implored women in her international best-selling book, *Le Guerilleres* (The Warriors):

*"There was a time when you were not a slave, remember that. You walked alone, full of laughter, you bathed bare-bellied. You say you have lost all recollection of it, remember. The wild roses flower in the woods. Your hand is torn on the bushes gathering the mulberries and strawberries you refresh yourself with. You run to catch the young hares that you flay with stones from the rocks to cut them up and eat all hot and bleeding. You know how to avoid meeting a bear on the track. You know the winter fear when you hear the wolves gathering. But you can remain seated for hours in the treetops to await morning. You say there are no words to describe this time; you say it does not exist. But remember. Make an effort to remember. Or, failing that, invent."* [1]

Anywhere you find a woman drawing outside the lines, stepping outside the lines, or living outside the lines, you are looking at traces left behind by the Wild Woman, still alive and remembered. Anywhere you see a woman who refuses to behave herself, who refuses to sit down and be quiet, you're looking at the Wild Woman who, instinctual creature that she is, has left her scent nearby for us to sniff out and remember her. Anywhere you encounter a woman, a mother, a daughter, an aunt, a grandmother, a sister, a wise crone taking on the establishment at her own peril, look no further. Wild Woman is standing before you, full of laughter and fresh from her "bare-bellied bath!"

This is our time to be the warrior woman; this is our time to discard the cultural inhibitions of "couldn't, wouldn't, shouldn't" that have kept us tied up in knots, too scared to take risks, too afraid we don't have what it takes to live our wildest dreams; too afraid to grab hold of our inner Wild Woman and proudly pull her essence over us like a long-forgotten magical cape we have remembered only in

---

1    Monique Wittig, *Le Guerilleres*, p. 95.

our dreams. As French feminist Wittig urged, we must remember those times when we were wild and free, or failing that, invent. As Swiss psychologist Carl Jung urged, we must dream the dream forward. As we reclaim and reconnect with those missing wild parts of ourselves, it is with a renewed vitality and bodacious assertiveness that we ask ourselves, what is the dream we want to dream forward? In order to create a new world of equality and respect for all, we must begin with our own inner transformation of remembering and re-connecting to our wild feminine. We must claim our innate wisdom and wildish natures that have lain in the underworld of our psyches for millennia, languishing, fretful, waiting, waiting, waiting like Queen Penelope, wife of the Greek hero Odysseus, who was forever weaving her tapestry during the day to ward off the unwanted, treacherous suitors that plagued her court and undoing her day's weaving by night, waiting until Odysseus would return.

Today's women of a wildish nature aren't waiting for Odysseus to return to save them. We've got a new vision; we've heard the Call of the Wild Woman and we intend to follow it wherever it leads. Like Ariadne in the Greek myth of Theseus and the Minotaur, who gives a ball of golden thread to the hero Theseus to mark his way and get safely out of the labyrinth before being killed by the Minotaur, we're taking our hard-won threads of gold and using them to weave new stories and myths that tell of women who are heroic, emboldened by the re-discovery of the richness of who they are. We're going to tell stories that remember who we are as wise women, wild women, strong women, brave women, smart women, visionary women and with these memories we will create the new cultural myths to guide us into the New World we have seen in our dreams and visions.

Let us begin this heroic journey to remember our Wild Woman natures waiting in our psyches to be reclaimed. This is our task now, to find her and take her back into the fullness of our being for she has much to teach us.

AS we mentioned, there are many places to search for the Wild Woman, but as writers, storytellers and every kind of magical woman who lives betwixt and between, we will begin our journey of discovery for Wild Woman by looking at three stories from three different cultures that speak of female deities of a wildish nature who demonstrate strong, powerful role models for us to learn from as we remember that we, too, are part of and contain within us this same wild essence.

## Artemis: Lady of the Wild Things

The first myth we'll consider depicts the Wild Woman archetype of the Greek Goddess Artemis. Artemis, often called Lady of the Wild Things, was the Goddess of the hunt, most often pictured dressed in animal skins with her bow and arrow slung across her shoulder. Although she was one of the twelve gods and goddesses who dwelled on Mt. Olympus and could have lived in magnificent temples or palaces, she preferred to live in the wilderness of the forest and mountain places where she delighted in using her animal instincts to survive. She traveled with her group of bare-breasted nymphs and the wild animals that accompanied them.

The bear was a special animal to Artemis. Fierce, independent and strong, the bear was an animal ally to many who followed Artemis. Young girls called "she bears" underwent an initiation into the bear clan of Artemis by spending time alone in the wilderness under the guidance of a leader. These young girl initiates roamed and hunted in the forests, learning the ways of animals and how to care for themselves in the wild. They were taught to be independent, physically and emotionally, and to rely on themselves and each other for support and survival. They wore bear robes and performed dances to honor their emerging animal natures.

## Untamed Instincts & Rage

There was a fierceness and passion in Artemis' nature that is both terrifying and magnetic. In a Homeric hymn to Artemis, the extent of her wild nature is described in this way:

*"…Over the shadowy hill and windy peaks she draws her golden bow, rejoicing in the chase, and sends out her grievous shafts. The tops of the high mountains tremble and the tangled wood echoes awesomely with the outcry of beasts; earthquakes and the sea also where the fishes shoal. But the goddess with a bold heart turns every way destroying the race of wild beasts; and when she is satisfied and has cheered her heart, this huntress who delights in arrows, slackens her supple bow and goes to the great house of her dear brother Phoebus Apollo, to the rich land of Delphi, there to order the lovely dance of the Muses…"*

Artemis is a powerful symbol for our untamed instincts. Just as nature has its own impersonal justice, so did Artemis. She hunted with a bold heart, "destroying the race of wild beasts" according to Homer.

Here we see glimpses of the wild aspect of ourselves that like Artemis is unwilling to be governed by laws that define, restrict or limit our behavior. Being a huntress and goddess over the animal world was symbolic of Artemis' role as ruler over the unconscious powers that still take on animal form in our dreams. Once we bring these images to consciousness, these animals can become our totem or spirit allies in journeys to the spirit world and can provide assistance and protection in our everyday life.

The untamed rage we see personified in Artemis can be a primary force and powerful ally *once we learn to recognize and focus its explosive nature.* One story that tells of Artemis and a young hunter named Actaeon accurately describes the shock and horror many women fear will occur if and when they express their anger. In the myth, the young hunter Actaeon is out hunting in the forest when he innocently happens upon Artemis and her nymphs bathing nude in a stream. Startled, Artemis becomes outraged at being discovered in her private place and reacts with a bloody vengeance by turning Actaeon into a deer, which his own dogs hunt down, tear into pieces and eat!

This untamed, wild instinctive nature also expressed itself through the women who followed Artemis, leading people to label them "berserkers" or "werewolves of the North." These "berserkers" were feared because of the animal frenzy that would overcome them, causing them to experience fits of madness, resembling the women who followed Dionysus who were also described as going temporarily insane, tearing bodies apart and eating them.

This wild, undirected primal energy of an Artemis Wild Woman is frightening and terrifying, especially to women who have veiled or repressed their anger or rage for long periods of time and fear the intensity of its release. They find it difficult to allow their passionate fiery side to express itself, but until they do, they won't learn how to direct or assume responsibility for it. As women, most of us are taught that anger is bad and that to express it is some sort of pathological behavior showing we're out of control or don't have it together.

Coming to terms with expressing anger or rage is every woman's personal and challenging journey as she learns to connect with her inner Wild Woman. This involves trusting ones self to learn how to express rage without harming self or others and to assume responsibility for its expression. This requires emotional discipline, self-awareness and practice, practice, practice; it may also require working with a therapist, shaman or medicine person to give us the support and guidance we require during this arduous task of accepting rage as part of who we are and learning how to express it in a responsible way.

## Claiming the Full Power of Our Instinctual Natures

In opening up to the reality that we possess both the power to destroy as well as the power to create is at the heart of re-claiming the full range of our instinctual natures. Disowning or repressing our dark, wild side only leads to our projecting it onto others. It is only when we trust ourselves not to destroy someone else by learning to recognize and be responsible for our own disruptive, cruel energy that we are safe enough to release our rage and fierceness without harming ourselves or others. As the "nice girl" persona begins to melt away in the newly emerging heat and passion of an archetype such as Artemis, there is the possibility for an integrated wholeness of self to take place. This work of integration and emotional healing is part of the Wild Woman Initiation and Resurrection section described later in the book.

Artemis was close to the wild nature of humanity and according to Homer, exemplified the "savage instinct-governed being who lived with the beasts and the free-growing plants." Numerous ancient illustrations, however, also show Artemis as a winged figure, indicating that she was also a heavenly being, not just a chthonic, meaning of the earth, goddess. "As goddess of opposites, she represents the whole, containing in herself the three realms that in Greek mythology were later shared by her sons, Zeus, Poseidon, and Hades." [2]

Artemis personified the teeming life of nature and universal motherhood. She was known as a virgin goddess, goddess of midwifery and fertility, though never of marriage. The Greek word "parthenos" that translates as "virgin" simply meant "not married" and unlike how the word is used today, it had nothing to do with a woman's body or sexual experience, which we'll discuss in more detail in later chapters. Women often called on Artemis to help them with childbirth or difficult deliveries. Her temple at Ephesus was one of the Seven Wonders of the Ancient World and her most celebrated place of worship. It was at Ephesus that the remarkable image of her as the many-breasted goddess was found. The magnificent, tall sculpture is composed of numerous heads of different species of animals that spring from the front of her body in a series of bands extending from her breasts to her feet and decorating her sides from the hips downward are bees, roses and sometimes butterflies.

---

2    Erich Newmann, *The Great Mother: An Analysis of the Archetype*, p. 277.

 WRITING EXERCISES

1.  Listening for and heeding the Call of the Wild Woman is part of a woman's journey to wholeness. The following writing exercises are meant to help you identify those times in your own life when you first heard that call and what you did or didn't do in response.

    > Were there important women in your early life such as your mother or a grandmother, aunt or teacher who encouraged you to be yourself, to not be afraid, to jump and run and yell as loud as you wanted; to splash in mud puddles, climb trees, get dirty or play baseball? Describe this person or persons and a situation with them where you felt it was not only okay to be yourself but that it was actually quite wonderful to be you!

    > Imagine a time when you were a young girl and were included in a circle of wise women elders who told you stories about a nurturing Great Mother being who loved you more than anything and was always watching over you. Describe what that circle might have looked like and how you felt to be surrounded by such great love and acceptance. Do you think it would have strengthened your sense of a wild self to know that it was okay to be every inch of who you were, inside and out; to be, in fact, a "woman who runs with the wolves" or other wild creatures?

    > Artemis had many animal allies. What animal or animals do you feel especially drawn to? How have they shown up in your life and did you ever feel their help or guidance during difficult situations?

    > Describe a time, place or a dream where you encountered your inner Wild Woman essence. What was that experience like? Were you scared, angry, numb, or did you feel empowered and excited at a happy reunion? Describe and draw or find images of what your Wild Woman looks like and put these in your journal. Imagine a conversation with her and write it in your journal. Title this part of your journal: *My Wild Woman*, or another title that comes to you.

    > Write about a time when your rage was out of control and you hurt someone. What were the results and what did you learn from the experience?

    > Write about a time when your rage saved you. What were the circumstances and describe anyone else who was there with you.

 ART EXERCISE

    > *"SHE-BEAR" ART EXERCISE.* Imagine that when you were a young girl you were a "she bear" initiate to the Goddess Artemis. What was your experience in the woods and what did you learn? Was there a similar experience in your own childhood that taught you how to live comfortably and safely in the woods and encouraged you to express and be proud of your wildish nature? After you've answered these questions, create a collage of yourself as a "she-bear." Use a photo of yourself as a child somewhere on the creation. Write about your process of creating this collage.

## Pele: Vengeful, Destroyer Goddess of Volcanoes

Spiritual ecology sees the spiritual and natural worlds as interactive and interdependent. This way of seeing the world is at least as old as shamanism, which reaches back some 20 to 30,000 years or more. Spiritual ecology is a practice or way of experiencing the interconnectedness of all life. It can involve and include meditation, ceremony, ritual, awakening of the physical senses, becoming aware of subtle energies, theater, storytelling, dancing, drumming, chanting, studying various wisdom traditions, vision questing, hiking and pilgrimages to scared sites and power places.

Can a place be sacred? If so, what makes it sacred? Are myths created or inspired by place? Can a place loose its sacredness? These are some of the questions we seek to answer as we follow a deliberate path in finding and remembering how our wildish natures, like all of earth itself was once considered sacred. In the Hawaiian Islands where the Goddess Pele makes her home, it is difficult to separate the land from the myths and stories told by native people. For generations past and present, the Hawaiian people have told the story of *Pele-honua*, Pele of the sacred land, and *Pele-'ai'honua*, Pele the eater of land when she devours it with her volcanic flames. Being an oral culture, Hawaiians tell her story through chants, or *mele*, and dance, or hula.

Pele is the Goddess of all the volcanoes of Hawaii. Sometimes in the stories she appears as a tall, beautiful young woman. In other stories, she appears as an old woman accompanied by a white dog. When enraged about something, she may appear as a woman of pure red flames. Her sacred spiritual name is *Ka'ula-o-'ke-ahi*, meaning the redness of the fire.

The ancient myth of Pele like that of Artemis provides us with another example of the untamed wild instinctual nature of the Wild Woman archetype. Pele was the daughter of Haumea or Hina, goddess of fertility who was one of the supreme or original goddesses in the ancient Polynesian homeland of Tahiti. According to Herb Kane in his book *Pele: Goddess of Hawaii's Volcanoes*, Pele didn't arrive in Hawaii until some time after the original gods and goddesses had already settled there. Like all Polynesians, Pele was a master sailor and came to Hawaii by sailing canoe from the islands of Tahiti around 450 AD.

Stories say she first landed in the northern islands of the Hawaiian archipelago and continued moving down the island chain through Ni'ihau and Kaua'i digging deep pits for her home where her sacred fires could be protected. But her angry sister Na-maka-o-Kaha'i had followed her and wherever Pele would dig a crater, her sister would deluge it with water. On the geologically older island of Kaua'i, the craters became wet swamps while her volcanic activity continued to move down the island chain to her present home on the still growing Big Island which saw major eruptions as recently as 2018.

This part of the myth coincides with the modern geological knowledge of shifting plates in which the Hawaiian islands were built in an assembly line as the ocean floor slid north-westward over a hot spot in the underlying layer of the earth's crust.[3] While many of the mysteries of Pele's domain have been explained scientifically, the spirit of Pele lives in the hearts and minds of Hawaiians through their stories.

---

3    Herb Kane, *Pele, Goddess of Hawaii's Volcanoes*, p. 13.

The awesomeness of an erupting volcano can hardly be explained in anything other than emotional or spiritual terms. To stand or be near Pele when she is erupting is to experience the very birth-making process of our Earth. It defies all scientific naming and explanation and puts one into a mixed state of euphoria and terror.

All the supreme gods and goddesses that first came to Hawaii from Tahiti were considered the ancestors of the people as well as all other living things that later emerged on the islands. Those who were most directly descended from these immortals were considered the chiefly or royal families and, like the ancient Egyptians and other royals throughout history, they struggled to keep their bloodlines pure so that the power, or *mana* as it's known in Hawaii, of these godly ancestors might flow through them unimpeded and thereby benefit their subjects.

## Power to Create and Destroy

Like Artemis and the ancient Goddesses of many cultures, Pele possessed the power to destroy as well as the power to create. To this day, however, native Hawaiians do not fear Pele but regard her as a relative, an *'aumakua* or ancestral spirit that takes an active role in the lives of all who live on her body, which is the land or the *aina*. She is affectionately called "Tutu" Pele, Tutu being the Hawaiian word for grandparent.

Similar to other primal cultures, early Hawaiians considered themselves and everything around them as inseparable from nature, with everything and every one being an integral part of the whole. For them, there is no word for "religion" since the sacred is part of every aspect of life.

Like other ancient cultures, there was a time in old Hawaii when *kahunas* or medicine teachers, priests and priestesses were responsible for the healthy relationship between the people and the land. This sacred relationship between the people and the land was also present, for example, in the beliefs of early Celtic tribes as seen in their myths of King Arthur, called the wounded Fisher King because of a wound in his thigh that symbolized fertility, indicating that his relationship with the land was out of balance, causing him and all the people to suffer.

Stories of Pele tell of a revengeful, jealous and violent goddess and none show her as beneficent or compassionate. Having personally stood numerous times on the edge of Pele's crater home in the Kilauea volcano of the Big Island, however, I have come to sense that the full essence of Pele is that of both Death Giver and Life Bringer; a being whose archetypal image represents the same powerful force as that of Black Goddess Kali of India who is highly revered, and also gives life as well as destroys it.

The old Hawaiian "religion" and gods were formally abolished by the monarchy soon after the death of King Kamehameha in 1819, although many disenfranchised priests and priestesses of Pele clung to their roles in open defiance of the new laws, while many others simply continued to worship Pele in secret.

## Pele: Vengeful, Destroyer Goddess

Here are two stories about Pele for consideration as a reflection of the untamed, raging Wild Woman archetype. The first story echoes that of the vengeful Artemis who turned the hunter Actaeon into a deer.

## Pele and the ʻOhiʻa Tree

Two young lovers, a man named ʻOhiʻa and a woman named Lehua, lived on the mountain slopes of Pele's domain on the Big Island. Pele noticed ʻOhiʻa one day and was attracted to him but he did not return her attention. Outraged at his rejection, Pele killed them both. She turned ʻOhiʻa's body into a tree that eventually became known as the ʻohiʻa tree, and his lover Lehua's body into the flower of the ʻohiʻa tree, the feathery blossom known as the luhua blossom. Today, the ohiʻa berries from the ohiʻa bush are sacred to Pele and are used as offerings to her in rituals and ceremonies and in the flower leis for the hair, especially when the hula is performed.

## Pele and the Detachable Vagina

The second Pele story is most unusual because it involves a woman's vagina and how it was successfully used as a powerful decoy. In this regard, it not only echoes the Sumerian Goddess Inanna's poetry extolling her wondrous vulva but also reflects other stories told about women in ancient Greece who, because they regarded their vaginas as having enormous power, would sit in their fields of growing grain and flash their vaginas, believing that this act would nourish the grain and the land, resulting in an abundant harvest.

One day Pele was journeying together with her sister Kapo when the pig god, Kamapuaʻa saw them. He was immediately aroused by the sight of Pele and began to pursue her. It just so happened that Kapo possessed a detachable vagina, which she took off and threw as a decoy away from the direction they were headed. The pig god Kamapuaʻa followed after the flying vagina, allowing Pele and Kapo to escape to the island of Oʻahu to a hill inland from Hanauma Bay named Kohelepelepe, which means detached vagina. To this day, the little hill still bears the imprint of where Kapo's detached vagina landed.

## The Land and Its Stories

That the land is sacred, has intelligence and possesses a voice of its own can be seen in the stories told throughout all oral cultures, and this is especially so in Polynesia. Ecologist and philosopher David Abram articulated this connection between people and an animate earth in his book *The Spell of the Sensuous*. According to Abram, primal cultures like those of the Hawaiian islands haven't "closed themselves within an exclusively human field of meanings and so still dwell within a landscape that is alive, aware and expressive…indeed, the linguistic discourse of such cultures is commonly bound, in specific and palpable ways, to the expressive earth."

Abram views language itself as having developed out of this kind of intimate relationship with the land. He believes that the linguistic patterns of an oral culture remain uniquely responsive and responsible to the more-than-human life-world or bioregion in which that culture is embedded. It's easy to understand, he says, the destitution indigenous people experience who have been forcibly displaced from their traditional lands.

To an oral culture, the relationship between the telling of stories and the land is never merely incidental because the events that unfold belong to the place and to tell the story of those events is to let the place itself speak through the telling. This relationship between story and place is more than an analogy to a deeply oral culture but is something they experience along with other animals, stones, trees, clouds, and volcanoes; all of which are regarded as characters within a larger story that is visibly unfolding all around them.

 WRITING EXERCISES

1. How was anger or its expression treated in your family? Write about your process in coming to terms with your anger or rage.

2. Describe a time and place when you experienced a "wild erupting of nature," meaning something that happened to you while you were in nature that allowed you to see that you weren't in charge. Did this experience shift your perspective on how the land and nature impacts your understanding and experience of having a physical body connected with everything around you?

3. Write about a time when you experienced a sense of awe or connection to a place that felt sacred to you. Describe in detail the setting and what you experienced.

4. Write about a time when you "yielded up your sane judgment" in a particular situation and something totally unexpected and wonderful happened.

## Kali, The Black One

A third cultural myth that also reveals the raging, untamed aspect of the Wild Woman archetype is told of India's Black Mother Goddess, Kali. She, too, is both a destroyer and giver of life as her stories testify.

Today, the terrible mother in the form of Kali, called the Black One, is the most exonerated Goddess in India. Her temple in Calcutta is famous for its daily blood sacrifices of animals in her honor. Innumerable works of Indian art as well as poems and stories attest to the devouring, negative aspect of this Universal Mother.

In one story, Kali stands in a boat that floats on an ocean of blood. Kneeling, she scoops the warm blood to her lips and drinks. Blood, symbol of the life force of the world of children whom she brings forth and sustains, she feeds back to herself. She is life feeding on life which she has created and which she can and does destroy. To many westerners who have been taught to honor only the good and positive aspects of a divine being such as those belonging to the Virgin Mary, this image of a devouring mother goddess is not only terrifying but also horrifying.

The two faces of Kali, the nurturing as well as destructive, are again revealed in a story told by one of her devotees named Ramakrishna, a nineteenth-century Bengali saint. Ramakrishna recounts a vision in which Kali appeared to him as a young woman of extraordinary beauty, who rises up from the Ganges River. Kali crosses to the shore where she gives birth to a baby whom she lovingly places to her breast and suckles. Suddenly, she transforms herself from a beautiful young woman to a terrifying, ugly hag who stuffs the child into her mouth, crushes it with her razor-sharp teeth and jaws and swallows it! Then she re-enters the water and disappears.

Stories of Kali such as these are terrifying; yet, her power to rage symbolizes a power we women need to recognize in order to develop, "the power to assert ourselves, to set our own limits, and to say "no" when necessary." Sylvia Perera in her book *Descent to the Goddess* compares Kali's dark domain to black holes, disintegration and decay, which are forces that devour and destroy, but as Perera tells us, they also incubate and bring forth new life. Since rage releases our spirit by pushing us through our illusions of powerlessness, contact with this archetype representing the dark side of the Wild Woman not only grounds and strengthens us but also provides the fire necessary for inner transformation.

### The Power of Destructive Energy to Transform

As shown in her myths, Kali's destructive energy can be transformative. The enormity of her transformational power is shown in two myths that speak of her as the dancing goddess. Kali's dancing represents her powers of creation and divine play. Often portrayed dancing with Shiva, Lord of the Dance, in one myth their dancing grows so wild and intense that the whole earth threatens to shake to pieces. The story goes on to tell us that if the earth should fall apart, the two immortals would simply create it again with another divine dance.

A second story shows Kali as she kills two demons, drinks their blood and begins a frenzied dance. Suddenly, she realizes she is dancing on the corpse of Shiva himself. Reminiscent of Isis who brings Osiris back to life with her life-giving breath, as Kali continues to dance, her energy flows into Shiva and he is brought back to life. In the Hindu tantric tradition, Kali's close association with Shiva reveals the nature of reintegration of our human and divine levels of existence; with the ultimate result of this union is our soul's liberation from the wheel of karma and its cycles of life and death. Kali, as Shiva's spouse, is identified with her creative and destructive energies and as such, her horrific nature is seen as a destroyer of the illusions of the ego. To the sage Ramakrishna whose poetry sang her praises, Kali is the benign mother of all.

Kali's abode is called "the island of Jewels" where her throne sits in a grove of wish-fulfilling trees and the beaches are of golden sand, washed by waters of immortality. Like Pele, the Hawaiian Goddess of Volcanoes, Kali burns red with the fire of life, while the earth, the solar system, the galaxies of far-extending space, all swell within her womb. She is the source of life and of everything that lives. She is also the death of everything that dies.

In Kali we see the dark Wild Woman archetype revealed in the fullness of her terrible beauty. She is at once a paradox of gruesomeness and tenderness, demonstrating that the creative as well as the destructive feminine principles are but different aspects of the one being and exist side by side. Both positive and negative poles are an inevitable part of our experience and life. Like Artemis and Pele, Kali provides a way to re-image and balance the beneficent aspect of the feminine with the destructive.

 WRITING EXERCISES

1. Describe your ideas for connecting with the Wild Woman's raw primal, untamed energy inside yourself. How might you take responsibility for taming and evolving this energy? You may want to imagine answering these questions within the context or template of a myth and a re-telling of your own life story; or, by re-writing a few significant scenes from your life showing how you recognized and experienced your primal instinctive nature in a responsible manner.

2. The myths of the three goddesses, Artemis, Pele and Kali, all demonstrate a beneficent aspect of the feminine archetype as well as a destructive one. Take some time to identify those two aspects in yourself and write about a time when you acted in accordance with both of these energies. Did the experience make you stronger or help you to feel more powerful about yourself? What are your thoughts regarding how these dualities can exist together? Do they create a paradox or do they both reside within the whole of a person's being?

3. Write about a time when you asserted yourself and stood up for yourself in a difficult situation. What were the results and what did it cost you? What were the benefits? Can you relate any aspect of that experience to Kali's fire to transform?

 ART EXERCISE

4. *MAKING A SPIRIT DOLL.* The bloody images of Kali with skulls hanging from a belt she wears at her waist are terrifying. This art exercise is intended to imagine her as an ally and protector by creating a Spirit Doll that embodies both these energies. First, gather a few visual images of Kali and sit with them for a while as you imagine what aspects of her that you want to incorporate into your Spirit Doll. Then gather the materials for the doll and her body. There are numerous ways to create her body, such as stuffing a sock with cotton, using a beautifully formed stick or piece of ocean driftwood; or you can purchase something from a craft store. Lay out all the things you've collected. Will you paint her face or glue some image onto her face area? Perhaps you'll make her face out of clay or cover it with a mask with only her red eyes peering through. Think about where you want to place her after she's completed...on an altar in your room, buried outside in the ground, burned in a ritual ceremony?

> Native people always speak of how they continually pray, sing or chant while they are creating their pots, rugs, paintings or Kachina dolls. Create your Spirit Doll with that same attitude of sacredness and purposefulness. Be aware of your breathing and your thoughts while you're creating her. Ask Kali to be present with you. Ask her how she would like to be represented.

> Once your Spirit Doll is completed, honor it with a special ceremony. Then, write about your process, from its inception to completion, detailing what you learned about yourself and the gifts of the Goddess Kali.

*Minoan Women.* From a fresco at the palace of Knossos, circa 1500 BCE
*Printed here under the Creative Commons Attribution-Share Alike 2.0 Generic license.*

# CHAPTER 2: Lost Wild Womanly Instincts

*Come to the edge. No, we will fall.*
*Come to the edge. No, we will fall.*
*They came to the edge.*
*He pushed them and they flew.*
~Guillaume Apollinaire

When did we stop trusting our instincts and why? How can we find what has been lost for such a long time? Where do we begin?

Notably, the first art and religions originated as reflections and celebrations of a Great Mother. Artifacts of the Great Mother have been discovered in India, the Middle and Near East, Eastern Europe and Greece. In fact, God was a female for at least the first 200,000 years of human life on earth. She was seen as the Great Earth Mother; or as analytical psychologist Erich Neumann called her in his book *The Great Mother: An Analysis of the Archetype*, she was Magna Mater. This Great Mother represented all of nature and was mother to the gods and goddesses who later took human form; and long before the oracle of Delphi in Greece belonged to Apollo, for example, Gaia, the Earth Mother was worshipped there.

Early humans acknowledged their awe and devotion to this Great Mother through their art, stories and rituals, which primarily focused on the female body with its miracle of birth and death like that of the Great Mother herself. Mystery rites and other religious celebrations grew out of women's experiences; their magical power to bleed and not die; their power to create and birth children of both sexes and their power to sustain their off-spring with milk from their bodies.

The first human images discovered in the Upper Paleolithic period (35,000 to 10,000 B.C.) were called the "Venus" figures. They were small figures shaped in the form of pregnant women and were made from stone, bone or clay. Very stylized in shape, the statues have no feet and their legs are tapered which allowed them to fit easily into the grave and cave niches where they were found. Although named after Venus, the Roman Goddess of Love, they are not sex objects as some archaeologists originally identified them; instead, they were depictions of the Great Goddess in one of her myriad forms, indicating abundance, fertility or birth and death. Sculptures of the later Neolithic period show amazing similarities in size, materials and shape to these earlier "Venus" figures and provide an important link between these two periods of time, attesting to their both having been goddess-worshipping societies.[1]

---

1    Merlin Stone, *The Paradise Papers*, p. 31.

## Women Discover Agriculture

Most historians agree that it was women who discovered agriculture about 10,000 years ago, resulting in the small clans that had once been nomadic to begin settling into small villages. Women, because of their close relationship with nature, were the ones who initially gathered wild plants for food and medicine, and eventually their observations led them to invent most of life's basic industries such as agriculture, food processing, preparation and storage, pottery, weaving, herbology, animal husbandry, language and the first writing, religious imagery and ritual. Women made precise observations of the cycles of the moon and were the creators of the first calendars. Most importantly to our inquiry here is that women were considered to be reflections of the Mother Goddess, and therefore, magical beings worthy of respect and honor.

This period of mostly peaceful co-existence for the goddess-worshipping people began to come to an end, however, when warring tribes from the Russian and Asian steppes, commonly referred to as the Indo-Europeans or the Barbarian hordes, began to invade the cultures of Old Europe, India and Mesopotamia, killing, raping and plundering entire villages, leaving total devastation in their wake. A notable example is that of the warrior Genghis Khan, c. 1162, and his fierce mongrel warriors numbering in the hundreds of thousands that thundered across vast expanses of the steppes, riding their wild horses and ultimately creating the Mongol Empire, the largest in the world before the British Empire. These warrior mongrels worshipped a Sky god who wielded a thunderbolt and had no interest in the Mother Goddess worshipped by the peaceful settled agrarian people whose lands they invaded and villages they destroyed. Over a period of several thousands of years, wave after wave of invading hordes came sweeping across central Asia, India and into Europe, leaving in their wake complete devastation, which eventually resulted in the entire civilized world collapsing and entering into what became known as The Dark Ages.

## Crete and Catal Huyuk

Knowledge of the existence of the worldwide worship of a Great Mother in pre-historic cultures has continued to expand as extensive archaeological discoveries have uncovered female figurines made of clay, stone, and bone as well as fragments of paintings found in caves and shrines thought to be sacred to a Great Goddess. We'll look at two ancient cultures where significant discoveries have been made that help us to understand the role of women in developing cultures and how their spiritual sustenance

Mural painting in the ruins of Knossos Photo credit: Arne Nordmann, Crete, 2004. *Printed here under the Creative Commons Attribution-Share Alike 3.0 Unported license.*

was sought in a Great Mother Goddess. We'll also look at what happened when those cultures were destroyed and women were relegated to slavery and became property of a male patriarchal hierarchy.

Bronze sculpture of an acrobat leaping over a bull's head, Crete, Minoan, about 1700-1450 BC, British Museum.
*Printed here under the Creative Commons Attribution-Share Alike 2.0 Generic license.*

Today, as research of early cultures has continued, discoveries at sites on the island of Crete and in the Neolithic city of Catal Huyuk in Anatolia (modern-day Turkey), it has become apparent that women of earlier times were greatly honored and respected. That peaceful societies existed in our distant past has also been one of the unexpected and life-affirming discoveries at these two sites. Excavations being done at the ancient site called Catal Huyuk where data was uncovered from examining ancient skeletal remains and thousands of female figurines were found, seem to support the idea that this society dating from Neolithic times was egalitarian, with no overt aggression or hierarchies, giving further credence to its having been a matriarchal or matricentric community

Craig Barnes, lawyer and author living in Santa Fe until his death a few years ago, has given a wonderful account of the beauty and significant contributions made to ancient civilizations by the people who lived on the island of Crete and the nearby village of Thera, or Santorini as it's known today. His book *In Search of the Lost Feminine: Decoding the Myths that Radically Reshaped Civilization* details the exquisite artwork focusing on nature that was created by the Minoan culture. The art work was found on urns, statues and wall paintings shows flowers, dancing women, playful dolphins, monkeys, and flying fish. On the walls of the palace of Knossos on Crete, for example, there are numerous frescos of nude woman vaulting on the backs of bulls, images of beautiful women with bare breasts, wearing snakes coiled around their arms and carrying bowls of fruit.

Barnes, as well as many archaeologists, have made special note that on Crete, as at Catal Huyuk, there have been no discoveries of weapons, no scenes of warfare and destruction, and no warriors brandishing weapons among the artifacts or on wall drawings anywhere, and further, that these two peaceful cultures were female-focused.

According to Barnes, one important reason to study ancient myths is because they reveal the origins of what he considered to be patriarchal propaganda. He details many of the ancient myths such as *Helen and the Trojan War*, which along with countless other stories began to move away from showing women or female deities as having power and status; instead, the myths were revised to show warring heroes and male deities such as Zeus being in control. This shift in power depicted in the revised myths coincided with the nomadic invasions as well as seafaring warriors and by the year 1200 B.C had reduced the entire Aegean world to rubble, plunging them into a Dark Age that lasted for over 400 years. When they finally emerged, cultures had become brutal, with stories that praised heroes, told of vengeful gods and a people that had become fearful of the divine and of death.

According to Barnes, by 800 B.C. women had become the target of widespread vilification. The new mythology that emerged after the Dark Age was now focused on the glorification of war; the idea of immortality was redefined and ecstasy was to be feared. It was the time of heroes and gods; according to Barnes, "the consequence of this new mythology was to bring heroes to the front and send decent women to the back rooms of the households, where they were not to be seen and not to have commerce with men who were strangers... At this same time women's sexuality was charged with dark foreboding and women were subjected to the twin requirements that they be either virgin or married, the sine qua non requirement of any patriarchal order."[2]

## Sexualization of Culture

During the centuries of Indo-European invasions and devastation to the goddess-worshipping cultures of our early ancestors, stories of the nurturing Mother Goddess were gradually repressed and replaced by stories of an all-powerful male deity who wielded a thunderbolt, as Barnes, Joseph Campbell, Robert Graves, Merlin Stone and others have documented. Amazingly, this new male deity also was credited with having created the world and all of humanity, without the assistance of a female counterpart.

How did it happen that things got so turned around as to attribute birth to the male of the species and the female was subjugated and left out entirely? It is here in those early revised stories that the first understanding of women's sexuality as something to be feared seems to have originated.

In a book called *Myth and Sexuality*, author Jamake Highwater, an award-winning Native American writer, says that it was through the knowledge of their bodies that our early female ancestors observed the difference between their bodies and that of the animals around them.

Estrus in animals meant they only mated one or two days in a month, whereas the human females didn't experience estrus, making a continuous sexual life possible. Highwater maintained that as long as women's mysteries were elevated over male authority, women were at the center of the "sexualization of culture;" and that the earliest mythologies supported and reflected women's cultural impact as well as assuring that the Great Mother was the dominant worldwide myth that supported the early primal paradigms of the world.

2    Craig Barnes, *In Search of the Lost Goddess*, p. 93.

Early myths focused on the powers of women, which according to Highwater, suggests that this unique sexuality of the female was a fundamental force in shaping human consciousness. He quotes cultural historian William Irwin Thompson who observed, "human beings have a self-consciousness which emphasizes sexuality, perhaps because the origins of human consciousness are somehow related to the origins of human sexuality. Humans are far more libidinous than beasts. They do not follow biological necessities; to the contrary, they have conceptualized sexuality. *And it therefore makes no sense to assume that sexual passion is the archaic heritage of our animal nature.* Contrary to popular opinion, it is our *passionate sexuality* that is the most human and the least animalistic element of our character. Female sexuality was the model of human sexualization and the initiator of the hominization of primates... woman is the creature who, with a unity of mind and body, moves from the estrus cycle to the menstrual cycle... the religion of humans is sexual, but out of the association of sexuality with the forces of nature, human females were to create our first religion, a religion of menstruation, childbirth mysteries and the phases of the moon."[3]

Highwater notes that although the reign of the Great Mother passed into oblivion long ago, during the thousands of years when her myth dominated the lives of our early human ancestors, she provided the foundations upon which human communities were organized, which still exist, despite the denial and rise of patriarchal values. The influence of the Great Mother remains in our mythic vision and influences our understanding of the world and ourselves.

 WRITING EXERCISES:

1.  In reading and reflecting on the evidence and myths that tell of our early ancestors who worshipped a Great Mother figure or archetype, what are some of the takeaways for you?

2.  Write an essay or personal narrative about your own ideas regarding how our original female ancestors may have been a force in evolving the consciousness of the human species, as well as how they have led us in developing our culture and ways of living on the earth.

3.  How has the repression of women and the figure of a female deity impacted your life and that of women today?

---

3    William Irwin Thompson as quoted by Jamake Highwater, *Myth and Sexuality*, p. 50.

## Reaching Back In Time For a Feminine Psychology

Esther Harding was a renowned psychotherapist, author and former student of the famous Swiss psychologist Carl Jung. Her book *Women's Mysteries: Ancient and Modern* written in the early 70s, made Harding one of the first women to focus on the modern psyche of women while also linking it to a historical background. To be more specific, her book was an attempt to present the archetypal foundation of a feminine psychology. By looking at the psychology of primal peoples, their mythology and the comparative history of early religions, her well-researched book sought to understand women's unconscious processes; specifically exploring how the psyche functions and how the archetype's pattern of behavior revealed itself, then and now.

Harding's mentor and teacher Carl Jung brought forth many new ideas, including the concepts of a collective consciousness and archetypes, which he brought to the attention not only to the psychological community but also to a wider audience interested in how the psyche works in human beings. Jung described an archetype as being metaphysical in its deeper meaning because it transcends consciousness. The psyche, according to his understanding, consisted not only of the contents of our consciousness as derived from our senses but also contained a person's ideas, which led him to the conclusion that one part of the psyche could be explained through recent causes but another part reached back to the deepest layers of human history. It was this reaching back into the earliest history of human beings and focusing primarily on the female, how she was seen at that time and how she evolved, that formed the intent of Harding's book.

### The Revolution From Within

In reaching back into historical times, Harding saw that civilization after civilization had succumbed to destruction, either from outside forces such as the centuries of barbarian invasions or from the decay and corruption from within. She argued that a new option was available to us moderns and could be achieved by bringing the undeveloped or neglected aspects of the individual consciousness into greater awareness and balance, thus creating what she called a revolution from within, making it unnecessary in her view to overthrow an entire civilization or culture.

Because women and their ways of being have been repressed for so many centuries, forcing them to adapt to roles requiring they ignore their inner instinctual natures and impulses, this looking within to both her masculine and feminine principles, requires that a woman turn to the discarded subjective material to discover what is "real" for her. To our ancient ancestors, this looking within was achieved through the embodied wisdom of their religious mysteries and rituals.

Harding says that in the past, an initiation to Eros, which she defined as the principle of psychic relatedness rather than love, was an essential phase of an inner development in the emotional realm. The feminine principle or essence has to do with relatedness or human relationships and can't be understood through the intellect or academic study. According to Harding, the reason men considered a woman so mysterious was their persistence in trying to understand her intellectually or rationally. She believed that it was at this juncture that we would be able to realize that the intellect alone isn't sufficient and necessitates turning to the unconscious realm, to study symbols and the instinctive ways of behaving for a better understanding of women and their relationship to the  feminine principle.

## The Feminine "Blood" Mysteries and the Moon Goddess

An ancient symbol for the feminine as distinct from the masculine that has remained constant throughout the ages is the Moon. The Great Mother had many names and faces and took many forms. In one aspect of her being, she was the Moon Goddess through whom women experienced their ever-changing cycles of nature. The moon was an ancient symbol that for many cultures represented the feminine "blood" mysteries. Knowledge of these "blood" mysteries was learned through initiation rituals to the Moon Goddess. All life and culture were believed to originate in women's "blood" mysteries, which were associated with the changing cycles of the moon. Since earliest times women were honored and held in awe because of the magical changes that occurred in and through their bodies. Women were not only highly esteemed because they were creators like the Great Mother herself but because they were also image changers. They could magically turn one thing into something entirely different, like making bread, for example, or turning water and clay into pots.

As Harding detailed in her book *Women's Mysteries: Ancient and Modern*, the Moon deity was originally seen by our ancestors as an animal, then later, as a god or goddess who was attended by animals and then still later, the animal attendants were replaced by human beings who wore animal masks and performed animal dances. The Moon Goddess was often shown wearing horns of an animal, often a cow, as her headdress. Harding suggested that the animal attendants and animal symbols found throughout the ancient goddess shrines could have served as a constant reminder to the worshippers of the wilder aspects of the goddesses' nature from which they had partly evolved.

According to Harding, in early civilizations, feminine instinct was perceived as entirely animal, as people observed the same fierceness of a human mother's care for her offspring and the same intensity of desire in the mating season, that was characteristic of both beast and women alike.[4] Harding thought that as humans evolved, however, women developed something nearer akin to the emotion we would identify as love, which allowed her to rise above her purely animal nature. The goddess was represented in the female form and although she had transcended to some extent her animal passions, she retained the fierceness of her feminine instincts by still riding her lion, giving birth to animals, wearing her headdress of cow horns and still being attended by her beasts.

---

4    This is a different interpretation than that quoted earlier by William Irwin Thompson who saw animal and human passion as being different in its origin and expression.

Women's bodies are attuned biologically and psychically to the moon. There was a time when people planted their crops by a moon calendar, understanding its ability to bring forth a favorable harvest and to avoid crops dying if planted too early or too late. Likewise, women's bodies bled in harmony with the moon's cycles that marked the passage of time, a time immeasurable by a linear calculation. Women "know" that silvery or golden orb we call the moon, because she inhabits our bodies and tells us when it's time to release our eggs of creation that we carry in our ovaries. Her cycles are our cycles. She is as much our mother as the Earth is our Mother. It is a powerful relationship and one that deserves our celebration.

Today, women are coming together again in healing circles or Red Tents, through earth-centered spirituality groups that perform rituals to honor the cycles of the moon and other significant seasonal events such as the equinoxes and solstices. Participation in these groups give women and men support and guidance for their lost feminine instincts and wisdom, much as they did in ancient societies when the Great Mother was worshipped and all women were honored and respected.

As women gather together in circles again to remember the ancient mysteries of the moon contained in their mostly long-forgotten "blood" magic, they dream and vision together. They drum, sing, dance, yell and cry. It is a time for mourning and grieving as well as celebrating. It is a time to acknowledge the innocence they leave behind with each new bleeding time. They nurture themselves so that they can nurture others.

 WRITING EXERCISES

1. What do you think of the idea of women's bodies and the feminine "blood" mysteries as being at the heart of women's instinctual power, both ancient and modern?

2. How does the idea of there being a direct connection to women's bodies and an energy dissemination from the moon during a woman's moon time, or menstruation, resonant with you?

3. It wasn't until the early 1970s that information about women and the presence of female deities in pre-historical times began to be published and made available to the general public. *The Language of the Goddess* by Marija Gimbutas an UCLA archaeologist was written after a lifetime of exhaustive research. In her book, she showed that the small statues and similar artifacts from ancient cultures did not represent simple "fertility cults" but represented the religious beliefs of cultures worldwide. In what ways does the knowledge of women's power in pre-historical times affect you? Do you feel empowered, neutral, or angry that this aspect of ancient history isn't taught to women and men?

4.  Collect art images of ancient goddesses, ancient symbols and other artifacts and create a collage of a real or imagined female ancestor. Then, create a story about your "real" or imagined woman; imagine what her life was like; what her name was and where and how she lived.

*Hades, God of the Underworld and the Goddess Persephone* from Spring Equinox Performance on Maui
Photo credit: Suzanne Canja

# Chapter 3: Healing the Split from Our Feminine Nature

*Daughters, the women are speaking. They arrive*
*Over the wise distances On perfect feet.*
*Daughters, I love you.*
~Linda Hogan of the Chickasaw tribe

In patriarchal literature, stories of the sacredness of a mother-daughter relationship don't exist. Christians celebrate the father's relationship to the son and the mother's relationship to the son but the story of mother and daughter is missing. Author and theologian Mary Daly in her book *Beyond God the Father* is quick to point out that the Virgin Mary was allowed only a son, but no daughter. What effect has this emphasis on the superiority of the male and the importance of male relationships had on relationships between women, especially the mother-daughter relationship? For women who have grown up in a patriarchal society where their very being has been devalued, there exists a wounding that goes beyond that of the personal mother-daughter relationship, which has to do with a rejection of our deep feminine nature, our core essence. One place to begin to recognize our wounded inner feminine is by understanding and reconciling the relationship with our mother.

A daughter because she is the same sex as the mother, seems a natural extension of her mother. This fact, according to Swiss psychologist Carl Jung brings with it a feeling of immortality because every mother contains her daughter in herself and every daughter, her mother, giving them an experience that every woman's life is spread out over generations. In spite of this almost inexplicable bond, however, as Simone de Beauvoir, French feminist, philosopher and author observed in her book *The Second Sex*, in a patriarchal culture, the mother-daughter relationship is severely unbalanced because the mother must give her daughter over to men in a male-defined culture where women are considered inferior. According to de Beauvoir, the mother must socialize her daughter to be subordinate to men and if her daughter refuses or challenges the patriarchal values, the mother is likely to defend the patriarchal norms against her own daughter, which creates a lack of trust, generates feelings of betrayal and makes a loving relationship difficult if not almost impossible.

Nowhere is this betrayal of the daughter by the mother seen more vividly than in the myth or fairy tale of Bluebeard. The naïve psyche of a Wild Woman, meaning a woman who has lost touch with her instinctive inner knowing, acts like a magnet in attracting a predator and that's exactly what happens in this story. Here then, is my adaptation of the French folktale as written by Charles Perrault. The story begins when a nobleman named Bluebeard begins to court three sisters.

## The Tale of Bluebeard & A Mother's Betrayal

*Once upon a time there was an ugly nobleman named Bluebeard, so named on account of the blue color of his beard. He had been married to many beautiful women all of whom had mysteriously disappeared.*

*Bluebeard begins to court three sisters by inviting them, along with their mother, for a picnic. He arrives in an impressive carriage pulled by horses wearing bells and ribbons. He feeds the women delicacies and tells them delightful stories; but the two eldest sisters remain skeptical of his good intentions; however, like her mother, the youngest sister is able to "look past" his ugly countenance and blue beard and convinces herself that he's not so bad after all. When Bluebeard asks the youngest sister for her hand in marriage, she immediately agrees, and once they are married, off they go to his magnificent castle.*

*One day Bluebeard has to go away on a trip but before he leaves he tells his new bride she can invite her family for a visit. "You may explore the castle at will," he tells her, handing her a ring of keys. "But never, never go into the room that this tiny key unlocks," he warns her before leaving.*

*When the young wives' two sisters arrive for a visit, she shows them the ring of keys and tells them of Bluebeard's warning not to open the door that fits the tiny key. As though it were a game, all three sisters set out to find which door the tiny key fits, finally coming to the last door to be checked, they insert the tiny key into the door's lock and to their delight it fits. With glee and excitement they swing the door wide open but the room is dark and they are barely able to see. Once their eyes adjust to the dim light, they behold a grim and grizzly site. Scattered around the room are the bloody body parts of Bluebeard's murdered former wives. The women scream and quickly run from the room, slamming the door behind them. The wife, seeing that the tiny key has blood on it, wipes it on her dress to clean it, but the blood won't come off. When the two sisters try to clean the blood off the small key, they too are unsuccessful. Nothing they do will clean the blood from the key.*

*Unexpectedly, Bluebeard returns early, and the sisters run and hide outside their younger sister's room while she quickly hides the bloody key inside her wardrobe closet.*

*"How did everything go while I was away?' Bluebeard asks her. "Good, good. Everything was good. My sisters were here and we had a good time."*

*"I'm glad you enjoyed yourself. Now please return my keys," he says.*

*She hands him the keys; that is, all but the tiny key. "Where is the tiny key?" Bluebeard demands.*

*"Oh, I put it in my clothes closet for safe keeping," the young wife lies.*

*"Shall we go and fetch it together, then?" Bluebeard asks. When she opens the closet, to her dismay, the key has dripped blood onto all her beautiful gowns.*

*"I see you have disobeyed me," Bluebeard screams. "Now it is your turn to suffer the same tragic fate as my other wives," he says, grabbing her by the arm and dragging her toward the hallway.*

*"Please, please let me have some time before you kill me to make my peace with God," she pleads, to which Bluebeard reluctantly agrees.*

*The young wife hurries to her room and onto the balcony where her sisters are hiding. "Sisters! Sisters! Bluebeard has found me out and wants to kill me. Do you see our brothers coming?"*

*Her sisters shake their heads and tell her, "We see some dust off in the distance, but that is all."*

*The young wife implores her sisters three times if they see their brothers coming down the road and three times the reply is the same.*

*Meantime, Bluebeard has grown impatient and yells, "I'm coming for you wife. Prepare to die."*

*Just as Bluebeard is about to kill his wife, her brothers arrive and brandishing their swords, slash Bluebeard to death.*

*The young wife inherits his fortune along with the castle. She uses the money to help her siblings and to bury the dead wives. Eventually she remarries to a man she loves.*

What are we to make of this gruesome tale and how does it relate to the mother-daughter relationship? In the fable, the mother happily goes on the picnic with her three daughters. One can only conclude that she, too, is impressed with the nobleman's money, fine horses and carriage, and of course, his castle. Otherwise, why wouldn't she have insisted her youngest daughter refuse Bluebeard's proposal of marriage since two of her eldest daughters have expressed their reservations about him? The mother makes no efforts to protect her daughters and gives them no instructions as to how they must trust their instincts to guide them. Instead, she encourages her daughters to ignore any misgivings they have towards Bluebeard, which ultimately leads her youngest daughter directly into the arms of a murderer. It is an extreme betrayal of the daughter by the mother based on a culture of male bias.

Like the three sisters in the story of Bluebeard, many women today are un-mothered, having received little or no nurturing or guidance as a child or young woman regarding their need to become aware of people and situations that are dangerous and could cause them harm. This abandonment by the personal mother has deeply wounded many women who continue to suffer throughout their lives, feeling they don't deserve kind and loving relationships or that they must do everything themselves. Many have difficulty asking for help and don't trust themselves to make wise decisions because they don't feel good about themselves and lack self-confidence. Many women aren't even aware that they hold themselves back in life because of negative messages they received from their mothers or other important women and men in their lives. Many women have no idea of how to protect themselves from predatory men or situations that are sometimes literally murderous. Nor are they urged to pay attention to their instincts in judging another's character or intentions and they definitely don't learn how to say "no."

Before we go blaming the mother for every misfortune, however, we have to remember that our mothers and grandmothers don't teach their daughters to be brave, to ask questions, to take risks, trust their gut or to forget all that "make-nice" behavior, *because they weren't taught those things either*. They, too, are daughters of the patriarchy, having grown up trying to please their fathers, husbands or bosses! As poet Adrienne Rich said, "the woman I needed to call my mother was silenced before I was born."

 WRITING EXERCISES

1.　How difficult do you find it to assert yourself and say "no"?

2.　Did you ever experience a betrayal by your mother or other female in authority? How has that impacted your life?

3.　Learning to recognize a dangerous situation is also clearly visible in the familiar fairy tale of Hansel and Gretel. In this story of a young sister and brother, they are lured into the house of a wicked witch who wants to fatten them up and eat them. Gretel recognizes the danger they are in and takes action by pushing the witch into the very oven she was heating up to cook and eat the two children. In this courageous act, Gretel leaves behind her childhood innocence, naiveté and "make nice" behaviors, all qualities women must sacrifice in order to grow into mature womanhood.

> Imagine you are Gretel. Describe how you felt before and after pushing the witch into the oven. Can you think of any similar situations in your own life where you "pushed the witch into the oven?"

> Write about any other qualities or attitudes you realize you would have to sacrifice in learning how to listen to your instincts?

## A Sacred Feminine Has Gone Missing

In her book *The Heroine's Journey*, author Maureen Murdock suggests that the mother-daughter split is really the split from one's feminine nature and that healing this wound goes way beyond a woman's personal relationship with her mother since it was caused in part by the extreme imbalance in values held by our culture. This skewed imbalance in values separates women from their feelings and spiritual natures, and leaves them lonely for deep connection. Murdock views this split from the feminine as something that requires an initiation into a feminine mythology by a mother or grandmother in order for a woman to develop a relationship to her inner feminine and to a Great Mother or Sacred Feminine; however, since most women don't have mothers, grandmothers or wise women elders to initiate them into a feminine mythology, women often seek initiations in other ways, some of them healthy and supportive, such as participation in circles of wise women, Red Tents, women's support circles where women are taught ways to reconnect with nature and each other in positive, life-affirming ways. Many women, however, who have no guidance get lost and begin to wander alone; often trying to destroy themselves and their hated bodies through drugs, personal body mutilation, starvation and "murderous" relationships.

Women's loss and grief due to un-mothering by their human biological mother goes deeper, however, because they also haven't been taught the existence of a Divine or Great Wise Mother, a being who is available to embrace them with unconditional, loving arms, or is there to offer them strength and guidance when they need it; a Divine Feminine presence who offers them a place of refuge and access to Her eternal Wisdom.

## You Can't Go Back

In contemporary Western culture and religion there is only the male god of Christianity. No female divinity survived or is included in the Holy Trinity. Maureen Murdock suggests that one reason women have desired to connect with images and stories of powerful feminine deities and heroines that existed in pre-patriarchal culture is because they help to heal their wounded psyches that often still function as repositories of "as women, you are less than" values. As women, it is important to remember our cultural roots and heritage as descendants of an all-powerful Mother Goddess who was worshipped for thousands of year; however, it is equally important not to get stuck in fruitless arguments about whose god or goddess is the "real" god and should be worshipped.

In fact, many women and men today don't seek fulfillment or redemption, refuge or salvation through any god or goddess, past or present and see no need to restore any aspect of a divinity; however, this doesn't negate the value of studying humanity's evolutionary cultural history. To engage with earlier cultures' art and myths is to learn from them and to ask ourselves, what did our ancestors do that brought their lives and communities to a better understanding of the world and of themselves? What led many of them to an understanding that when everyone benefits, life is sweeter and easier? Answers to these and other questions are helpful in learning from their mistakes and incorporating what they did do that was beneficial. After all, we are the only species that still kills each other off in alarming numbers, often sanctifying the murders of others by claiming, like the Crusaders did when heading out on the First Crusade in 1095, "Deus Vult" or God Wills It.

In re-examining earlier cultures that benefitted from worship of a female deity, most women are not seeking to de-value men or kick out the male deity. One of the most reassuring discoveries that examination of the earliest goddess-worshipping cultures has shown, for instance, is that when belief in Magna Mater existed, all people, all creatures, all of nature's rivers, mountains, and forests were considered sacred. This doesn't mean that atrocities weren't committed when a goddess was worshipped. They were. Yes, our early female ancestors were given a somewhat higher status in those cultures but men were also honored.

## Two Very Different Myths

The two following myths show how early cultures regarded women in extremely different ways. The first myth comes from patriarchal times and tells of the devalued status of women in a play called *Agamemnon* written by Greek playwright Aeschylus which gives a horrific account of how King Agamemnon sacrifices his daughter Iphigenia in hopes of creating favorable winds to take the Greek ships to Troy, where they will fight and defeat the Trojans and bring the wayward Helen of Troy back to Greece.

Here are a few verses from the play *Agamemnon* that describe the horror of the sacrifice and of King Agamemnon's decision to go ahead with the hideous deed in spite of his daughter's devotion to him:

*"Heavy is my fate, not obeying,*
*And heavy it is if I kill my child, the delight of my house,*
*And with a virgin's blood upon the altar Make foul her father's hands.*
*Either alternative is evil.*
*How can I betray the fleet? And fail the allied army?*
*It is right they should passionately cry for the winds to be lulled*
*By the blood of a girl. So be it. May it be well."*
*Whatever the cause, he brought himself to slay*
*His daughter, an offering to promote the voyage*
*To a war for a runaway wife.*
*Her prayers and her cries of father,*
*Her life of a maiden counted for nothing with those militarists;*
*But her father, having duly prayed, told the attendants*
*To lift her, like a goat, above the altar*
*With her robes falling about her,*
*To life her boldly, her spirit fainting,*
*And hold back with a gag upon her lovely mouth*
*By the dumb force of a bridle*
*The cry that would curse the house,*
*Then dropping on the ground her saffron dress,*
*Glancing at each of her appointed*
*Sacrificers a shaft of pity,*
*Plain as in a picture she wished*
*To speak to them by name, for often*
*At her father's table where men feasted*
*She had sung in celebration for her father*
*With a pure voice, affectionately, virginally,*
*The hymn for happiness at the third libation....*
*To learn by suffering is the equation of Justice; the Future*

*Is known when it comes, let it go till then.*
*To know in advance is to sorrow in advance*
*The facts will appear with the shining of the dawn.*[1]

## WRITING EXERCISES

1.  How does reading a story in which women were so little valued make you feel? Do you think women's status throughout the world has changed that much?

2.  Was there a time or situation in your life when a male figure betrayed or hurt you? Did you tell anyone? How was the information received?

## The Myth of Demeter & Persephone: A Loving Mother-Daughter Relationship

There is another much older myth that tells of a loving relationship between a mother and daughter that is still available to us today to assist in understanding and healing not only our relationship with our personal mothers but also with our inner feminine nature.

*The Myth of Demeter and Persephone* tells the story of two Greek Goddesses who were mother and daughter. According to this ancient Greek myth, Demeter possessed a passionate love for her child, her daughter Persephone, which gives us a way to reimagine the power of the feminine through the celebration of a mother-daughter relationship.

There are two versions of the story; one is a pre-patriarchal version that was told and celebrated before the repression of the worship of the Goddess and before women were devalued. The second version was written and revised during patriarchal times by the poet Homer, around the seventh century B.C. There are written records of Homer's version, making it the better known of the two, so we'll look at it first.

### The Story of Demeter & Persephone As told by Homer

*One day the lovely Mother Goddess Demeter leaves her daughter Persephone to play with friends in a flower-filled meadow. Persephone spies a narcissus flower in lavish bloom, bearing an intoxicating scent, "which beguiled the maiden." As she reaches to pick the flower, "the wide-pathed earth yawned" and Hades, Lord of Death and the Underworld, appears from the depths riding his immortal horses, and sweeps her away into the underworld where he rapes her, afterwards declaring that she will be his Queen of the Underworld.*

---

1    *Agamemnon* by Aeschylus in *Ten Greek Plays*, edited by L. R. Lind, p. 43.

When Demeter returns to the meadow and finds her daughter has disappeared, she is grief-stricken and roams the earth for nine days and nights, neither eating nor caring for herself as she searches for her missing daughter. On the tenth day, the Goddess Hecate arrives with a torch and offers to go with Demeter to find Helios and plead with him to tell them who stole Persephone away. Helios answers that it was Hades, brother of Zeus, but urges Demeter to cease her lamentations because, he tells her, this is a good marriage for your daughter.

Demeter turns away, more grief-stricken than ever and continues to wander until she comes to the town of Eleusis and there, while sitting by the town well, she meets the daughters of the local king and queen who ask her to be the nursemaid to their new-born brother. Demeter agrees. During her time of sitting by the well, she has also met an old woman named Baubo whose crude sexual jokes and flashing of her genitals causes Demeter to laugh for the first time since Persephone's disappearance.

The young son of the king and queen grows strong under the care of the Goddess, but one night the queen mother enters the room while Demeter is "passing the son through the fire-like brank (grain)" an act intended to bestow immortality on him. Horrified at what she thinks she is seeing, the Queen snatches him from Demeter's arms.

Angry, Demeter immediately reveals her radiance and who she is, and rebukes the Queen for denying her child the chance for immortality. This is a significant moment for the Goddess because it is at this instance that she "remembers who she is." She commands that a temple be built in her honor at Eleusis and once it is finished, Demeter sits alone inside and continues to mourn her daughter.

Meanwhile, everything on earth has begun to whither and die, and no one is making offerings to the Gods and Goddesses. One by one, they visit Demeter, plying her with gifts and pleading for her to return fertility to the earth, but she refuses to do anything until her daughter is found.

Finally, Zeus sends the messenger God Hermes to his brother Hades in the underworld telling him that he must release Persephone to Demeter so she will restore growth to the land. Hades agrees and tells the grieving Persephone that she is free to go. In parting, he offers her a pomegranate seed, which she eats. By eating the seed, Persephone has ensured her subsequent and yearly return to the underworld; for only if she had eaten nothing in the underworld would she be free to never return. Consequently, for one third of each year thereafter, she will have to return to the underworld during which time the earth above will lie fallow.

Amidst much rejoicing Persephone and Demeter are re-united. Hecate, too, comes and kisses Persephone and promises to be her "queenly comrade." With Persephone's return, symbolizing her true resurrection from the underworld, spring erupts upon the land once more. Demeter instructs the town's leaders regarding the hidden meanings of all that has happened and tells them how certain rites are to be carried out in the secret mysteries to be celebrated in her honor at Eleusis, celebrations that continued for over 2,000 years!

### The Older Demeter and Persephone Myth

More recently, author and feminist Charlene Spretnak gave us a pre-patriarchal version of the Demeter-Persephone myth in her book *Lost Goddesses of Early Greece*. In Spretnak's pre-Olympian version, it is the Goddess Persephone herself who actively decides she must go to the underworld for her own transformation and to help lost souls in their underworld journey. Obviously, this is a very different telling than Homer's version where Persephone is abducted by Hades and taken by force into the underworld, raped and kept captive. In Spretnak's research into an older version of the myth, Persephone takes on the responsibility for her soul's evolution by choosing to descend into the underworld, an intentional choice involving great personal sacrifice, which she deliberately makes to be reborn into a new and more complete understanding of herself. In this older, pre-patriarchal version of the myth, the initiation of Persephone into the darker aspects of herself is symbolized by her trip to the underworld while she is watched over by her mother and several other mature Goddesses.

 WRITING EXERCISES

1.    Almost every woman who has heard either version of the Demeter-Persephone myth has immediately commented with surprise at the enormity and depth of love shown by Demeter for her daughter Persephone. Unfortunately, most women can't seem to imagine such a mother's love. Is it difficult for you to imagine such a deep love as the one that existed in the mother-daughter relationship shown in the myth of the Greek Goddess Demeter and her daughter Persephone?

2.    Often after daughters become mothers, they have a better and more appreciative relationship with their mothers. What has been your experience of your relationship with your mother as you have matured and become your own person?

### Contemporary Re-Enactment of the Demeter Persephone Myth

While living on Maui, a group from *WomanSpirit*, a non-profit organization for the healing and creative arts, came together each spring for several years to do a re-enactment of the Demeter/Persephone myth in a beautiful outdoor setting. Adapting our text from Spretnak's book *Lost Goddesses of Early Greece*, the actors donned elaborate masks and costumes and acted out the Greek myth. The drama, performed in an outdoor setting amidst the beautiful Hawaiian tropical flowers and greenery, was a rite of renewal for the community and the land. It also introduced people to the story of a loving mother-daughter relationship, strong female characters and the male god Hades being in service to Persephone.

*Votive marble with Demetra and Kore* from Eleusis Museum. 470-450 BC. Photo credit: Davide Mauro.
*Printed here under the Creative Commons Attribution-Share Alike 4.0 International license.*

# Chapter 4: Rites of Passage: Maiden, Mother and Crone

*We have to make myths of our lives.*
*It is the only way to live without despair.*
~from *Plant Dreaming Deep* by May Sarton

As we saw in the last chapter, the myth of the Greek Goddess Demeter and her daughter Persephone tells about a time when celebrations were held in which women were specifically recognized and honored. Their story represented the belief in a Triple Goddess: maiden, mother, and crone. Demeter, Goddess of Grain and Harvest, was always pictured on tablets and reliefs with her maiden daughter Persephone, or Kore, meaning maiden. In these representations, Demeter, the mature mother, was often shown holding a fruit or sheaf of grain in her hand while Kore, the virgin-maiden, held a flower.

For 2,500 years before the birth of Jesus and the subsequent mystery rites belonging to a dying-resurrecting male god had begun to be celebrated, the ancient Greek myth of Demeter and Persephone portraying a loving mother-daughter relationship was celebrated in the ancient town of Eleusis. The Eleusinian mysteries celebrated the holy grain mysteries accorded to Demeter and her daughter Persephone and Demeter's recovery of "lost" Persephone, symbolizing the eternal cycles of birth, death and regeneration. To the ancients, it was Demeter's annual grieving at the loss of her daughter that caused the death of the crops. When she at last finds Persephone, there is a renewal of all life, signifying that the cycle of springtime has finally arrived.

By the 13th century B.C. Demeter was worshipped throughout all Mycenae and Greece but the early Christians who were much opposed to any secret rites to the Goddess, destroyed her temple at Eleusis in 396 AD, one of the largest shrines in Greece. To many, however, the site remained sacred and ceremonies honoring Demeter and her daughter continued well into the Christian era.

## The Maiden

The maiden was also known as Birthing Woman. The very first sacred site was thought to be the birthing circle. The Birthing Woman was put in the center of the circle of women who chanted, sang and drummed to help her deliver her child safely and with the full support of everyone.

According to Monica Sjoo, feminist artist and author, Birthing Woman was the original shaman because our ancient kin saw giving birth as a major initiation. Every Birthing Woman encounters the very real possibility of death as she brings forth new life through her body. It is through the act of giving birth that a woman has the opportunity to face her fears regarding life and death. Giving birth is a major rite of passage for the maiden and remains an initiation experience.

Today, many women who give birth in hospitals may be heavily sedated and barely have memory of the experience; or, their birthing experience, no matter how caring and attentive the midwife or doctor may be, it is still regarded as a hospital procedure and may not be regarded as a sacred rite of passage or initiation. Often a woman may schedule her time for delivery for the sake of convenience, and choose to have a cesarean section.

## Blessed Art Thou

The biggest lie on the planet for the past 2,500 years and more is the one that says women are in need of redemption because of being the vehicle through which evil entered the world; a distortion of the Eve and Adam story and of eating the forbidden apple in the Garden of Eden. The ancient Biblical myth says that because of Eve's transgression, the god Yahweh put a curse on all women that they would have to suffer in childbirth. Rather than seeing the pain of giving birth as a curse, but seeing it as an initiation, changes the story from one of banishment and shame to one of empowerment. A woman is the blessed one because she is born into a physical body with the secrets of the universe already built-in. Regardless of the shape of her body or the state of her mind, she carries inside her the very mysteries and natural flow of all life. Rather than being cursed by having been born a female, she is blessed.

Through the blood experiences inherent in her woman's body, a woman has no choice but to bleed as a young girl, which she does in natural rhythm with the monthly changing phases of the moon. Being born in a woman's body gives her the extraordinary advantage for becoming more fully balanced and consciously aware of the cycles of life. Although cycles seem to naturally happen to her, she has to work to become aware of them and of the enormity of the miracle that she simply embodies because she was born a woman.

A woman's path to self-fulfillment and wisdom is to fully know and accept that she is a being full of grace and miracle, and always has been. Men got the lesser role of the two because his ticket to wisdom doesn't lie inside the blood mysteries of the body, so in a sense, he has to make up a lot of stuff to do in order to approximate what women already have available to them by virtue of the female body, once they take notice. That's why there are male heroes and hero journeys and quests and all that sort of thing. Think about it. Men have to work their butts off to even begin to get to the experience of surrender to things outside their control, which is the beginning of wisdom, whereas a teenage girl takes it full on when she first bleeds! Not only does she master surrender to something that's beyond her control, but also she bleeds and doesn't die! Talk about a super hero in the current context of animated super heroes with powers over life and death!

Anywhere from age nine to thirteen years a girl will begin to bleed whether she likes it or not. Liking or not liking has nothing to do with it. Bleeding happens! Then the hormone race is on and, seemingly whether her head likes it or not, she wants to give birth to an offspring.

You look at all those "so and so begat so and so" in the Bible and behind each of those hundreds of men's names mentioned there, you will always find a woman...a woman who one month didn't bleed;

a woman whose blood and body were used to create a living human being from the flesh of her flesh. No wonder early humans made their first images in the shape of a voluptuous female being whom they probably worshipped and at the very least held the deepest reverence.

After a young female maiden has experienced her first monthly bleeding, has become pregnant by whatever means and given birth, she becomes a mother. Become a mother! Contrary to a few radical feminists and nay-saying others, giving birth is a super big deal! Many women and people in the health-care professions do regard giving birth as an initiation of a special kind. It's the Vision Quest, the Dark Night of the Soul, the Shamanic Soul Retrieval Journey, the Sweat Lodge, the Sun Dance, the Tibetan and Egyptian Books of the Dead, <u>all</u> the initiation processes rolled into one. Not only does a woman literally face death when she gives birth, but her body becomes the vehicle for another life to enter into this world! Her body! She uses her body to make another life out of a few microscopic cells and then she uses her body to push that tiny life out of her womb into a new world separate from herself. Let us all sing a verse of the Hallelujah chorus, not for a risen savior, but for the Birthing Woman. This is big stuff. Miracle stuff! And, at the same time, ordinary stuff. It's Great Mystery at work.

While I despise the hypocrisy and righteousness of the political right wing, right-to-lifers, surely, hopefully, somewhere inside all that rhetoric and hyperbole, there lies a love, a genuine respect and awe for life and at the same time, for the woman who makes this possible. Just as there is surely a love for all life among those women who choose to abort their fetuses for personal or spiritual reasons. To accuse these women of being murderers is ludicrous and smacks of the same kind of hysteria and fanaticism that resulted in the witch trials and mass murders of women accused of having congress with the devil during the Middle Ages; however, we women must be extremely careful with the gift given to us of the miracle of life that can grow inside our wombs. It is perhaps too little valued by some individual women and giving birth is certainly not honored by the greater culture of humanity at large. It's simply what women do and have always done. Would it be different if men were the ones who gave birth? As an old joke from the second wave of feminism said, "If men could give birth, abortion would be made a sacrament."[1]

There are many layers of meaning here and it's up to each of us to search diligently for the truth in our own lives and experiences and speak out when and wherever too much of our freedom is demanded to calm and appease those with contrary views who wish to control women's bodies.

 WRITING EXERCISES

1.  Over time women's rituals such as those celebrating the myth of Demeter and Persephone were repressed. Women's instinctual nature and her ability to heal were ridiculed, forbidden and declared unlawful. This repression signaled the beginning of the time when the Wild Woman, the archetype that contains and reflects women's instinctual natures, began to go missing.

---

1   When I turned 65 and became eligible for Medicare, I was bemused to learn Medicare routinely covers medications for erectile dysfunction.

> Imagine yourself and your mother attending a ritual celebrating the mother-daughter relationship. Describe what that ritual of celebration might look like. What would the conversation with your mother or daughter be? Who else would be there to help celebrate? Describe the setting? If this exercise is difficult for you, write about that.

2. Write about a time when you expressed an emotion or did something that your mother ridiculed you for doing. Describe the situation, what happened and how you felt. If this is still a painful memory for you, think about a possible way you could move through and past it while remaining true to yourself.

3. Recall a time in your life similar to the scene when Demeter is holding the Queen's infant by the feet and passing him through the fire to make him strong; a time when you had your *feet held to the fire like a sword* that is strengthened in the blacksmith's fiery furnace. What happened as a result? Think of a situation in which you had to stick it out in spite of pain or agony that resulted in your becoming or doing something extraordinary. Did your mother ever insist you do something that you resented or hated but that turned out to be good in the end?

## The Mother

The loss of a daughter or any creation for an older woman signifies the beginning of the loss of her own youth. In the myth of Demeter and Persephone, Demeter's challenge is not only to release Persephone to her destiny and womanhood but also to discover the meaning of the second half of her own life. She must release her carefree youth and turn inward to search for the mystery of the crone or her wise woman self. She must confront the personal rites of passage leading into ripened maturity and eventually, into old age. It is a dark and difficult journey of introspection and disintegration, often bordering on what feels like a kind of madness before it can transform into a type of visionary power and new creation during life's last cycle.

For an older woman, this rite of passage is played out not only in her psyche but also in her body through menopause and post-menopause. It is a time for grieving the passing of her youth and for her journey into the unknown land of the old woman or crone. The ego yearns to return to the past, to the status quo, to a former time when everything didn't sag or wrinkle. Like her daughter Persephone, Demeter too must pass through death to a new spring. It is an inner renewal that she must seek, however, one which knows no "age" only a heightened consciousness of life's never-ending cycles in which each one has its gifts and challenges. She can take comfort in knowing that seasons come and go; and that bound-up in the eternal cycles of change is a great wisdom to be learned.

When the Goddess mother Demeter sits alone in the temple she has ordered built in her honor, she enters fully into the sorrow of the great mystery or rite of passage into old age. It becomes the sacred ritual of a life yielding to what it cannot change and making peace with that knowledge. During her grief-filled nine-day search for Persephone, nine being the length of time to carry a child to its birth, Demeter has carried a burning torch, symbol of the eternal fire or light of our soul, which perpetually guides us. On the tenth day, Hestia or Hecate, crone goddess of the Hearth and keeper of the sacred fire in the temples of the Goddess, appears bearing her own torch to assist Demeter on her journey. Hestia is the comforter, the wise elder who bears witness to certain sacred events and rites of passage in our lives. Hestia remains a symbol of the deep bond between women as the sisters, mothers, and friends whose shoulders we cry on and whose arms and hearts open to embrace us and share in our sorrows and joys.

Goddess Demeter in *Re-Enactment of Demeter & Persephone* myth from *Spring Equinox Performance* on Maui
Photo credit: Suzanne Canja

A critical part of the myth occurs when Demeter "remembers who she is." A very necessary part of this rite of passage for Demeter and for women facing into their wise crone cycle is to remember who they are; an act that immediately releases them from their suffering and grief. As they reflect and seek to integrate their past with the present and extend themselves into the last cycle of life, perspectives shift, and become broader and more encompassing. Their views are more comprehensive, more inclusive, more "allowing" of different viewpoints and situations. They make peace with the fact that they don't know all the answers, or even most of the answers. They now become aware of their heightened sensitivities, of their willingness and knowledge that they are both the dancer and the dance. They do indeed wear a "new" face, but it isn't one given to them under the knife of plastic surgery; rather it is a face that reveals their essence; a face that they wear with satisfaction because their wrinkles tell their story, tell how they have passed through life's many cycles
of hardship, sorrow and loss with grace and forbearance; it bears witness to a dignity and fortitude of spirit that is theirs alone.

### A Personal Mother-Daughter Story

As I have grown and matured in my own life, different aspects of the myth of Demeter and Persephone have been important guides in my understanding of that most difficult relationship between mother and daughter. Like any good drama, the story has multiple layers that only reveal themselves after much living and reflection over time.

I first began to immerse myself in my own mother-daughter story one summer some decades ago after my daughter had left home to begin her own life. I was living in Taos, New Mexico and all summer long had picked wild strawberries on a steep slope a few hundred yards from my house, reminiscent of Persephone picking flowers in a beautiful meadow. During a visit from my daughter, who was now living in California, we were outside relaxing and sitting together in the wild strawberry patch.

The strawberry leaves, once a bright green, were rapidly turning celery-gold, orange and red. I realized that only a few short weeks remained until fall's first frost, to be followed much too quickly by the winter snows. I felt a pang of loss in my heart at feeling summer's vibrancy and delights slipping away into another of nature's ever-changing cycles. I thought about the cycles of change in my own life from being a daughter to now being a mother who was watching her own daughter become a woman.

What kind of mother was I being for my daughter, I wondered?

Had I done enough to prepare her for the time when she, like Persephone, would make her journey into the underworld to face the dark goddess, the archetypal Wild Woman whose instinctual nature would have to be encountered in her most terrifying aspects? Tears began to sting at the corners of my eyes.

"What is it, mom?" my daughter asked.

"I feel sad sometimes that everything changes so quickly," I replied.

"Do you feel like you're getting old or something?" she asked with her habitual coyote humor, putting her arm around my shoulders.

"A little. I feel all these changes in our lives so deeply. You're becoming a grown woman now and…" I said, my voice faltering and tears running down my cheeks.

"It's all those deep feelings that make you such a good writer and a great mom, and my best friend, too," she said, squeezing my hand.

Later as we hugged and embraced goodbye, I fought back my tears as I saw tears rolling down her cheeks. There were no words to describe the feeling in my heart as I drew her to me and kissed away her tears. My heartbeat quickened and my breath caught in my throat as I responded to the beauty and tenderness of another human being who called me "mother." I thought back to a passage in Nor Hall's book *The Moon and the Virgin* about the mother-child relationship.

*She carries the fruit of the night for nine months in her body. Something grows. Something grows into her life that never again departs from it. She is a mother. She is and remains a mother even though her child dies, though all her children die. For at one time she carried the child under her heart. And it does not go out of her heart ever again.*[2]

As I watched my daughter drive away, like the Goddess Demeter in the myth who grieves for her daughter when she disappears, I am filled with grief and a sense of loss. I know I must let my daughter go to her own life, to her own unique journey, just as I must go forward to mine. This giving up of a child, or a piece of art or anything we have created is very painful, but necessary to make room for the new. Even so, there is a palpable throbbing, an aching from the empty space inside my womb and my heart. Will I be able to embrace the next cycles of my life like Demeter did when "she remembered who she was?" Will I let my fears hold me back?

---

2     Nor Hall, *The Moon and the Virgin*, p. 97

 WRITING EXERCISES

1.  In the Navajo or Dine culture, there is a beautiful ceremony celebrating a young girl's first blood, called *Kinaalda* that represents her crossing from being a child to a young woman. It includes a special meal prepared in her honor and a special dress created for her to wear. The ceremony is based on the myth of *Changing Woman* and like *Changing Woman* the young initiate's hair is washed with suds made from the root of the yucca plant, followed by the young initiate's grinding of corn to make a large cake for the Sun. Prayers are sung and the young girl initiate is "molded" like *Changing Woman*, by her family as they gently place their hands on her head, eyes and feet to shape her into a beautiful, strong woman. Afterwards, all the people from grandmother to small babies stand in front of her to be touched and shaped by her hands that have become holy.

    > Write about your first blood, or menstruation. Was there a celebration of any kind? Who was there to help you celebrate? Were you treated special in any way? If the memories of your first blood are painful or especially sad, imagine a different set of circumstances in which you were honored and feted in amazing ways that let you know how special you were and acknowledged that you were a young woman.

2.  Various psychologists have explained that part of healing the mother-daughter relationship involves being able to see your mother not as some god or goddess but as a mere mortal with flaws and inadequacies. Releasing her from the role of someone who is all-powerful and all knowing is the first step in allowing her to be a human being who did her best, and allows you the opportunity to forgive her for the times when she failed you. It also allows you to learn how to nurture your own self, to become independent and strong, someone who doesn't need her mother's approval for how she lives her life. Write about how some of these ideas have played out in your life.

3.  Write a letter of forgiveness to your mother or daughter for any wrongs you feel they may have done to you. After you've written the letter, write about what you learned or felt during the letter-writing process; what was easy or what was difficult; what emotions came up for you while writing the forgiveness letter; what unresolved feelings still exist? Because this is a sacred healing ritual, make sure you write your forgiveness letter on beautiful paper written in your own handwriting.

4.  Write a short piece detailing what you imagine a healed relationship with your mother or daughter might look like. Maybe you see yourself in some sort of fun activity or ceremony, enjoying each other's company.

## The Crone

Author and psychiatrist Jean Shinoda Bolen offers us a new perspective on the word "crone" in her book *Crones Don't Whine: Concentrated Wisdom for Juicy Women*. She thinks it's time to redefine and reclaim the word crone from being a disparaging name for older women to one that denotes a crowning inner achievement of the third phase of life. She says that to be a crone is to be concerned with inner development, not outer appearance and describes a woman with wisdom, compassion, humor, courage and vitality.

Because this phase of a woman's life has been so overlooked and rejected, we will consider this rite of passage into becoming a crone, or wise elder, in its own chapter coming up next.

# Chapter 5: From Wild Woman to Wise Woman

*I will launch myself into death*
*like a bird taking flight for home.*
~from *You're Not Old Until You're Ninety* by Rebecca Latimer

Becoming a mature wise woman is the third and final cycle of the feminine "blood" mysteries that define a woman's life. Over her lifetime, a woman will come to know herself and her world through the "blood" mysteries she has experienced in her body. These natural states of being will have provided her with an involuntary flow and affinity with all of life. One of the phases of becoming a mature, wise woman or crone, is to recognize she has the ability to self-fertilize herself, much as female creators of the earliest myths did when they singly bore all life from their bodies into the world. These very early creation myths called the female the Divine Androgyne. Awareness of being capable of self-fertilization happens gradually once a woman no longer bleeds but instead retains the wisdom of the blood inside her body, which she can use for building and creating in new and profound ways never before dreamed or considered possible. Awareness comes that the blood is the essential carrier of wisdom just as the heart is the abiding place of love.

## The Third and Defining Act: Enter the Crone

Another level of learning occurs when a woman is left alone, literally or metaphorically, to contemplate what it means to be a mature woman, a crone, and what it might mean to grow older in a gracious manner, meaning not becoming too bitchy. A little bitchy seems to come naturally with the territory and when expressed in moderate amounts, enriches the journey.

A post-menopausal woman by definition is beyond childbearing capabilities, but becoming wiser about things doesn't necessarily happen with age. When I began to move into my crone cycle, I was with a young lover twenty years my junior, almost young enough to match my energy and liberal values, or so I told myself. I was still having an occasional bleeding time and when he declared that he wanted to have a child with me, to my later horror and disbelief, I seriously considered it! Obviously, it was time to "get thee to the temple of the grieving Demeter and remember who I was." So the Greek myth of Demeter tells us, once Demeter retired to the temple she had ordered to be built in her honor and had come to terms with her grief over the absence of her daughter Persephone, she began to consider what it meant to have a child who was now capable of being a mother. She began to ponder what it meant to be and become an older woman who no longer could bear children. Finally, she began to consider what she was going to do with the rest of her life.

For an older woman to daily see the body morph into a form clearly unrecognizable as the prior "I" she once knew; to daily experience the shape shifting of her body into new and highly unusual forms is a challenge. What kind of wisdom could one possibly glean from such a bizarre experience of daily witnessing the decay and breakdown of the physical body? I remember thinking at the time I was with my younger lover that if a Goddess like Demeter who had the power to fertilize and cause all things to grow on the face of the earth, that if she couldn't handle aging, what chance in hell did I, a mere mortal, have of aging with any kind of dignity or grace?

## The Importance of Remembering Who You Are

The challenges of accepting and loving a deteriorating, aging physical body can be enormous, but gaining wisdom from this process lies somewhere else. The dawning of wisdom at this point in the story of Demeter happens while she is sitting all alone in the temple built for her when she begins to remember who she is. Quietly. Slowly. She begins to *remember who she is*. The story doesn't talk about her weaving anything, or making anything, or mucking about with anything. She just sits quietly and alone in her temple remembering who she is.

She thinks about it for a long, long time. Who knows how long? It doesn't matter how long, either. It takes whatever time it takes, just like a baby in the womb takes however long to grow and be born...seven months, nine months... my first child was ten months in the womb!

Roe LiBretto, in her studio at age 63, creating *The Transmutation of Sacrifice*, a watercolor on wood panel, 32 x 80 inches. Photo credit: Jonathan Grimes.

Things have their own time and it is in the wisdom of surrender to those things outside our control that we begin to be able to comprehend some of the mystery of being a woman, and to sink down into a feeling of comfort that knowing and embracing a reality that exists beyond our control brings to us. We don't have to know everything. We don't have to be smart. We don't have to do anything but lean into the thing, embrace the thing whatever it is, and love it and ourselves as hard and passionately as we can. Because it's the loving of the thing that gives us the strength and eventually the wisdom to be gracious and accepting while embracing the changes to our bodies and our lives. It's the love that eventually fertilizes us and brings us back to ourselves and remembers us to ourselves.

As an elder, it took me years of celibacy to begin to deeply understand that I didn't need a man to stimulate me to the highest levels of creation of which I was capable. Of course, I was familiar with all the ideas and books of how women don't need men in order to feel or be complete and of how a woman has her own inner male or masculine principle residing in her psyche. But I tell you; it has taken me a long time to really begin to understand these ideas in the depths of my soul. I talked about them for many years before I could finally walk them; before I was able to embody the idea of a woman being able to stand fully alone and not be angry or dismissive towards men; to be a woman who is complete in her own radiant wisdom; to be able to stand alone and be complete with a heart full of love, bursting with compassion, and know, really know, that she could do it all, be it all, alone. Then, finally, to fully understand that once she has mastered standing alone in the fullness of her glory, she can stand, or lie with or be with another or many others, if she so chooses, and then, and only then is there the possibility of equal partnering, respect and honoring because she has remembered who she is.

I believe that we all know everything we need to know to get to the state of remembering that says all we need is love; that all we are is love. We are enormously invested in making everything complicated Everything is complicated and complex, but the beautiful paradox is, the opposite is also true. We are enormously simple! The crone cycle of the woman's blood mysteries brings all these understandings to her simply, or complexly, through the vehicle of her body. Her wisdom has been procured, if you will, through her body and accumulated over her lifetime. She receives all she needs to know to be a wise elder through her body, but she has to learn to listen to her body, with gentleness and respect, just as she has had to do through every other cycle of her blood mysteries, first as maiden then as mother and finally, now as the crone.

## What Is Wisdom, Who Has It and How Do We Get It?

Wisdom speaks to each person or creature in the tongue that only they can understand. It is not a universal language like Love. Love can be shared by touching bodies together or by singing songs into the wind while camping by rivers and wild places. Wisdom, however, uniquely expresses herself to her individual listeners, instructing them on how it is that embracing a wisdom path means we must act towards one another with loving kindness; but we get into all kinds of trouble once we think our "wisdom" should to be everyone else's wisdom and truth. From this perspective it's only a stone's throw away to righteousness and we all know how that feels if we've ever experienced a Seventh-Day Adventist's knocking on our door and we made the mistake of letting them in to "share" the word and Wisdom of God with us! It feels yucky and off, and frankly, sucks because there is no genuine dialogue, only preachy phrases like "we have the only truth and you'd better listen up!"

## Ideas or Information Is Not Wisdom

Jungian therapist Helen Luke has some interesting ideas regarding the Demeter-Persephone myth. She takes as her point of departure the later, patriarchal version of the myth by Homer which as we saw in the last chapter's telling of the myth, Persephone, or Kore as she was also called, is captured and carried off by Hades, god of the underworld, and raped. Luke sees the rape of Kore as the violent breaking of her virginity, but thinks it was necessary to retrieve the maiden Kore from her "passive state of being protected into the vital passivity of opening herself to receive the seed of the male…The Lord of the Underworld is he who arises, bursts forth from the unconscious with all the tremendous power of instinct. He comes 'with his immortal horses' and sweeps the maiden, the anima in a man, from the surface life of her childish paradise into the depths, into the kingdom of the dead---for a woman's total giving of her heart, of herself, in her experience of her instincts, is a kind of death."[1]

I used to be quite stimulated and took great comfort in Luke's and other Jungian ideas; but as I have grown older, I have less time and attraction for the glamour of elaborate and complicated systems of thinking and perceiving. I only seem interested these days in observing my breath for short periods of time each day, feeding and listening to the birds sing outside my window, doing a bit of writing and gardening and learning how to sing and draw again, if the lessons are short. What does it mean then, when all the mental fancy dancing and intricate two-steps have lost their appeal? For me personally, it signifies a breakthrough and freedom from a mind that has been held prisoner for decades by the glamour of ideas: new ideas, strange ideas, and well-articulated ideas—IDEAS! Give me a good idea any day and I could make a meal that lasted for months, maybe even years! Not so much anymore. Actually, I miss that. I relied on those ideas to give meaning to my life; to explain everything I couldn't understand about the world. Ideas were my shield and could buffer me against experiencing the world first-hand; without ideas there was no second-skin to get in the way of direct knowing and perceiving of the world through the senses, through instinct. Ideas are not real, though they can produce real things in the real world when acted on, and so forth and so on, and so forth and so on. You get the idea!

Which brings me back to the subject of "blood" mysteries. Blood is not an idea. Blood flows in our woman's body and outside our bodies. As women we bleed for thirty or forty years once a month and don't seem to be any worse off for having done so. Certainly, we don't die. We stop our blood when we're pregnant and use it to form the baby's body inside our wombs. Then, when we become older, we stop bleeding entirely and something else happens. We enter fully into the Temple of the Crone to contemplate, not the blood mysteries, but the Wisdom Mysteries, which were originally ruled over by the Goddess of Wisdom, Sophia. And in case you didn't know, being wise doesn't mean you can't be sensuous or in Jean Shinoda Bolen's word, "juicy."

Recently, I discovered a just-so story that has different understandings and outcomes of what aging can be. The story is based on an Athabaskan Indian legend, and features two old women as protagonists. Velma Wallis of the Athabaskan tribe in Alaska wrote down this legend, which became her first book, called *Two Old Women*. The story tells of two old women who were turned out by their tribe during a brutal winter famine to fend for themselves, but like any good story, it evolves into something much more complex and memorable, as all good "teaching stories" do. Here is my adaptation of Wallis' beautifully written story.

---

1    Helen Luke, *The Perennial Feminine*, Parabola, Volume V, No. 4, issue on Woman, p. 15.

## The Story of Two Old Women

*Once upon a time there lived a small band of nomadic Indians called The People, who lived in the far-flung Alaskan wilderness. The previous few winters had been brutal and although they followed the herds of migrating animals that were their primary food source, with so many mouths to feed and no relief from the bitter cold, their food supplies had depleted and many women and children were suffering and had died from starvation.*

*In the band were two old women who had been cared for by the People for a long time. Upon arriving at a new campsite, the younger men would set up the old women's tents and bring them water and wood for their fires. The younger women would haul the elder women's possessions from one camp to the next, and in return the old women would tan animal skins for them.*

*Although no one reprimanded them, the two old women were constantly complaining about one thing or another, but that all changed one day. On the eve of fast-approaching winter, the chief called the small group together and announced that because of so much suffering and starvation, they were going to have to leave the old ones behind. Leaving older members of the band behind in times of extreme starvation wasn't unheard of, and the two old women, Ch'idzigyaak, who had seen eighty summers, and Sa', seventy-five, had seen that very thing happen when they were younger. Nevertheless, the two elder women sat in stunned silence around the campfire, holding their chins up high, feigning pride and confidence to hide their shock. But no one protested the chief's decision. Not even Ch'idzigyaak's daughter or young grandson.*

*As the band gathered their things to move away, Ch'idzigyaak's daughter, with sorrowful eyes that seemed to beg her forgiveness, left a bundle of thickly stripped raw moose hide at her mother's feet, which had many useful purposes. When no one was looking, her grandson left a hatchet of sharpened animal bones in the branches of a spruce tree for them.*

*Soon the band of famished people left, but the two old women continued to sit by the campfire, humiliated and angry. They were angry because they were not near death; they were not blind; they could still walk; they had much life left in them. How could their people have left them to die like this? Sa', seeing that her friend was despairing, urged her on by saying, we can't just wait here to die. It is a long time before we are ready to leave this world. They think we are old and useless, but if we are going to die, let us die trying, not sitting here and letting the cold and hunger take us.*

*And so the two old women began what would be a year of determination to "let us die trying" during which time they put to work their multiple decades of experience and knowledge of how to survive. They began by gathering sticks for firewood and fungus from the fallen trees to keep the fire smoldering, and that very first night, in spite of their weariness and trauma of being left behind, they forced themselves to build some rabbit snares, which they set out.*

*Initially, during the long winter nights that followed when their survival was never assured, the two elders sat inside their shelter of caribou skins and talked at length about how they had let themselves become like children; how they had just stopped working even though their bodies were still healthy and could do more and yet they had chosen to use their time to complain, to never be satisfied. They realized that they had allowed themselves to become burdens on others and although they felt much bitterness and anger, they knew they had not helped their family and The People as they could have.*

*Through the long winter nights they told stories of their remembered youth and although their hearts remained heavy at having been abandoned, they began to realize that they would be able to survive if they were careful and worked hard.*

*And so it was, night after night, day after day, they used their wits, their hunting skills for trapping small rabbits, foxes & squirrels and over time, collected and stored large caches of dried meat and fish; used their knowledge of how to build shelters and how to stay warm; hauled wood from the deep forest and piled it around their cache and shelter and as their second winter approached, they were more than prepared. They used their time in the long winter evenings to sew fur mittens, hats and coverings for the face. They worked tirelessly and their bodies grew hard and strong again even though they felt lonely and missed their people.*

*Meantime, The People had traveled far from the camp where they had left the two old women, searching for game and food to eat but time after time their luck had gone against them and now, their clothes in tatters and their faces gaunt and thin, in desperation they had returned to the place where they had abandoned the elders the winter before. The chief remembered how sad he'd been on that day and during their travels, had fought the urge to return to save them.*

*But why had he brought The People back to the very place where they had left the two old women? They all looked around as though expecting to see them but there was no sign of them anywhere. After they had set up camp, the chief ordered Daagoo, a guide who was considered an elder even though he was much younger than the two old women, and several younger hunters to go to any camps nearby and see what they could find.*

*The chief wasn't sure if he was wasting time on such a futile effort but one thing he knew for sure was that during hard times The People should stick together and that last winter they had not done so. He had observed that The People had suffered in silence every since that day when the two old women had been abandoned. If they found the women, then that would give The People a second chance to make amends.*

*As Daagoo and the young hunters began to search the nearby camp areas, they found nothing. It wasn't until several days later that Daagoo caught a light scent of smoke. They walked in several different directions to track down where the smoke was coming from when they came to an area that even though the snow was untrampled and no campfire burned, Daagoo sensed that the two old women were alive and close by. He yelled their names out into the cold night air and waited for a reply.*

*Ch'idzigyaak and Sa' heard their names being called out in the stillness. The voice identified itself as the guide Daagoo. Could they trust him? They sat a long time deciding what was the best thing to do, finally deciding that they couldn't run any longer. They called back, "we are here."*

*When Daagoo and the young hunters came to the campfire, the two old women were waiting outside their shelter, with spears in their hand, like warriors. Daagoo immediately assured them that they meant them no harm, and "the chief sent me to find you."*

*Noticing how tired and weary the men looked, Sa' invited them inside their spacious and warm shelter where she offered them dried fish to eat. As the men looked around, they were astonished at how well and healthy the two old women looked while they, the strongest of the band, were thin and on the edge of starvation.*

*Daagoo told them that The People were starving and had little food left. "The chief is sorry and The People, too, for what was done to you.*
*Sometimes when times are hard, some will get scared and become mean, same as I did when we left you behind, but I tell you that I will protect you with my own life if that ever happens again."*

*As Daagoo looked at the old women, he realized that he had once thought them weak and helpless but seeing their strength, resilience and determination that had seen them through the hard winter, he knew he would never think that he was too old or too weak for life ever again.*

*Finally, after hearing more stories about how The People, especially the children, were in such poor health and some starving, the two old women told their terms to Daagoo for rejoining the group and for sharing their abundant store of food and other supplies. Soon, Ch'idzigyaak met with her daughter and forgave her, and in time, good relations were regained with all The People. They learned that they had thought themselves strong, yet had been weak, while the two old women whom they had thought were helpless and useless had proven themselves to be strong and resourceful. Now, The People began to seek out the advice of the two old women and to learn new things from them. In this way, they showed the two old women the respect they deserved and the two old women knew they would never think of themselves as weak and useless again.*

 WRITING EXERCISES

1.	Write your response to the story of *Two Old Women*. Write about any ideas of dread, fear or repulsions you may have about growing older, or if you're already a crone, how did this story impact what you already know about yourself and the aging process as you have experienced it?

2.	Are there some similarities to this story and that of Demeter & Persephone that you noticed? Have you forgotten who you are at your deepest and most powerful level of being? How might you "remember who you are?" Imagine yourself sitting inside the Temple of the Crone. What do you see happening?

 ART EXERCISE

3.	*A CRONE'S MANIFESTO.* Write your ideas for *A Crone's Manifesto* in your journal or create a separate art creation drawn from your own life or that of an older woman, mother, aunt or grandmother. You may feel inspired to create a journal or art piece illustrating the three phases of a woman's life: maiden, mother and crone.

4.	According to author Jean Shinoda Bolen, exceptional men can also be crones. She also says that when crones join together they can change the world. What do you think of these two ideas?

# Chapter 6: Wild Woman's Initiation

*It was already late enough, and a wild night,*
*And the road full of fallen branches and stones. But little by little,*
*As you left their voices behind, the stars began to burn through the sheets*
*of clouds, and there was a new voice which you slowly recognized as your*
*own, that kept you company as you strode deeper and deeper into the*
*world, determined to do the only thing you could do—determined to save*
*the only life you could save.*
*~from* The Journey *by poet Mary Oliver*

What do we mean by initiation in the context of finding and re-connecting with our Wild Woman nature? Initiations always have to do with something spiritual, usually denoting a symbolic death and rebirth experience. To reconnect with the Wild Woman archetype requires us to undergo a journey to the underworld of our deep psyches for our own initiation.

Most of us are familiar with the concept of the hero's journey brought to our attention through the work of mythologist Joseph Campbell. According to Campbell's book *The Hero's Journey,* the male hero sets out on a journey or quest and along the way must confront some terrifying force, person or impossible situation that requires him to perform powerful physical feats in order to complete a certain task. Along the way he will meet helpers, allies and mentors to help him complete this seemingly impossible task, often called the ordeal, as well as face many dangers and enemies who will try and stop him.

Ultimately, if the hero succeeds, he will return home a changed person who will share with his community the hard-won treasure or elixir that he has fought hard to win.

Does a woman's initiation differ from the classic male hero's journey, which we are more familiar with, and if so, how? Unlike a male on a hero's journey, for a woman, her heroic journey is often an inner journey where she must confront her inner demons or voices that tell her she isn't good enough, doesn't have what it takes, or numerous other debilitating, entrenched thoughts about herself she must overcome to find her own truth and understanding. In learning to overcome these inner as well as outer obstacles put in her way, the heroine must show extraordinary feats of courage, inner strength, and most of all, must learn to trust her feminine instincts to warn her of dangers that might prevent her from completing her initiation and how best to proceed when she is threatened. Author Maureen Murdock in *The Heroine's Journey* says that a woman's journey to find her authentic self is more of a circular path instead of the linear path traveled by the hero on his journey. On the circular path, the heroine will re-visit certain issues or challenges over and over again, taking time as she goes to integrate what she has already learned while becoming aware of what she still needs to know.

To heal the wounded wild woman we must regain a conscious relationship with our own inner feminine. In order to do that we must make our own heroine's journey, one that requires a descent into our deepest psyches, later to re-emerge, and in author and Jungian therapist Sylvia Brinton Perera's words, "restructured, reborn in an inner process and connected to the full range of feminine instinctual patterns." According to Perera in her book *Descent to the Goddess: A Way of Initiation for Women*, the ancient myth of the Sumerian Goddess Inanna provides a model for women living in our contemporary times "to go down to meet her own instinctual beginnings, to find the face of the Great Goddess, and of herself before she was born to consciousness, into the matrix of transpersonal energies before they have been sorted and rendered acceptable."

## The Descent Myth of Inanna

The oldest descent myth of initiation known to us is called *The Descent of Inanna,* which tells the story of the ancient Sumerian Goddess Inanna. According to Samuel Noel Kramer, the premier living expert on Sumer, the Myth of Inanna was inscribed on numerous tablets dating to 1750 BC and had lain buried and forgotten for almost a thousand years. It wasn't until an archeological expedition in the 1890s that the tablets were discovered in the ruins of Nippur, Sumer's spiritual and cultural center, near modern day Iraq. Over several decades Kramer spent time translating the original clay tablets and later, with the help of folklorist and storyteller Diane Wolkstein, working together they published a book called *Inanna: Queen of Heaven and Earth: Her Stories and Hymns from Sumer*. In the *Cycle of Inanna* the two authors tell of Inanna's life from adolescence to womanhood and finally, to goddess.

*Ishtar on an Akkadian seal,* Oriental Institute Museum. Photo credit: Sailko. *Printed here under the Creative Commons Attribution 3.0 Unported license.*

Inanna was originally an Earth Goddess of fertility and subject of some of the most erotic poetry ever written. Over time she became known as the Queen of Heaven, the same title that centuries later was bestowed on Mary, the Mother of Christ. Inanna was also known as the goddess of death and rebirth. Throughout the Middle East, specifically in Babylon, she was known as Ishtar; in the Bible, she was referred to as Ashera or Astarte.

The myth of Inanna predates similar tales that eventually spread throughout the Near East and the Mediterranean telling of a virgin goddess whose *son-lover*, a term explained in more detail below under the *hierogamos* ritual, suffers a sacrificial death and is ritually reborn after the goddess goes in search of him in the underworld. In all the ancient stories, the entire population mourned the death of the *son-lover* while on his journey to the underworld and sang praises and hymns of joy to greet their risen god when he returned every spring. It's easy to see the influence of this ancient myth on later stories, which many scholars see as a re-telling of this original story.

Here is the myth of the Goddess Inanna as adapted from *Interpretations of Inanna's Stories and Hymns* by Diane Wolkstein and *The Myth of the Goddess* by Anne Baring:

*From the Great Above to the Great Below*
*From the Great Above she opened her ear to the Great Below.*
*From the Great Above the goddess opened her ear to the Great Below.*
*From the Great Above Inanna opened her ear to the Great Below.*
*My Lady abandoned heaven and earth to descend to the underworld…*
*She abandoned her office of Holy Priestess of Heaven to descend to the underworld.*
*In Uruk she abandoned her temple to descend to the underworld.*

Inanna decides she must visit the dark realm belonging to her sister Ereshkigal, Queen of the Underworld.

"While I'm gone below to visit my sister," she tells her personal attendant Ninshubar, "wait three days and if I haven't returned, contact my father to come search for me."

Inanna prepares for her journey by gathering to herself the seven me, or laws, which are transformed into her ceremonial adornment: her royal crown, her jewels and robe. Thus arrayed and carrying her royal staff, she sets out alone on her journey to the Underworld.

Seven gates lead to the Underworld and demons guard each gate.

They ask Inanna why she has come. "I've come to see my older sister Ereshkigal and to witness the funeral of her husband, Gugalanna, the Bull of Heaven."

The Underworld is a dry, dark realm that Ereshkigal did not choose to rule but was given her for her domain. When she sees Inanna at her gates bedecked as the Goddess of Love, she is enraged at Inanna's glorious radiance and jealous of her freedom to move about as freely as she desires.

Ereshkigal commands the keepers of the seven gates to take Inanna's royal attributes from her, and so at each gate Inanna is forced to give up one after the other of her royal ceremonial adornments. When she finally arrives in the Underworld, she is completely naked. Ereshkigal focuses her eye of death on Inanna, declares her guilty and orders her body to be hung on a pole where her flesh begins to rot.

After three days when Inanna doesn't return, Ninshubar seeks out Inanna's fathers for help but they all refuse. Finally, Enki, the god of Wisdom, has compassion for his daughter and sends two creatures called the Galla to plead for Inanna's release.

*The Galla find Ereshkigal who represents the dark side of Inanna moaning in pain and in labor. It is this labor or "call" to be reborn that Inanna had heard from the Great Above. The Galla plead with Ereshkigal for the release of Inanna and she agrees. Once Inanna is reborn in the Underworld, she wants to leave immediately, but it isn't that easy.*

*If Inanna wishes to return,*

*She must provide someone in her place...*

*Inanna returns to the Great Above with the Galla by her side to make sure she finds someone else to take her place in the Underworld. While Inanna has been away, her two children and faithful servant Ninshubar have mourned her absence, but not so her husband, Dumuzi. He, who was once a Shepard but is now the King of Sumer because of his marriage to Inanna, has gone on with life as if nothing has happened.*

*Inanna finds Dumuzi seated under the very apple tree where they'd once made love, dressed in the noble me, garments Inanna has given him. He has not wept for his lost wife nor does he run to greet her.*

*Someone must go to the Underworld to replace Inanna and who better than Dumuzi, husband of Inanna, King of Sumer. As King of Sumer, he has been extolled by the Sumerians as all-powerful, wise and compassionate. If he is to be a truly great king, then he too, must journey to the feared place, to the Great Unknown, to the Great Below.*

*Dumuzi is filled with terror as the Galla seize him and carry him away to the Underworld. Inanna weeps profusely at her loss and of the sacrifice of her son-lover-king. The king has now entered the Underworld where he will be renewed in feminine wisdom and inner strength to take over the leadership and vitality of the country. From now on, for half the year the goddess Inanna and the king Dumuzi will be united; and for the other half they will be separated. For half the year, Dumuzi will actively rule over Sumer and will join Inanna on the sacred marriage bed, a ritual all Sumer will join in celebrating. The milk will flow in the sheepfold, the wheat will ripen and the apple trees will blossom. As the seasons change and the harvest passes, Dumuzi will enter a period of inactivity, quiet and meditation and will return to Ereshkigal in the Underworld.*

*Inanna's journey to the Underworld brings a new world order to Sumer. Once Inanna is restored to life, she ascends like the moon after its three days of death to assume her right place as the Queen of Heaven.*

*My Lady looks in sweet wonder from heaven, The People of Sumer parade before the holy Inanna*
*Inanna, the Lady Who Ascends into the Heavens, is radiant.*
*I sing your praises, holy Inanna.*
*The Lady Who Ascends into the Heavens is radiant on the horizon.*

## Initiation Rites to the Moon

Various scholars, psychologists and mythologists have interpreted Inanna's myth as a great lunar drama since she was originally worshipped as the Moon Goddess. This interpretation sees the story as telling or marking the phases of the moon. Inanna's descent represents the darkening phases of the moon and the appearance of the new crescent moon, symbolizing its rebirth after the three days of darkness.

*Lunar Eclipse.*
Photo credit: Marjorie St. Clair.

Inanna's descent story, however, is not only a dramatization of the ancient rituals associated with the moon cycle that influenced human consciousness for many thousands of years, but it is also a story of Initiation. Inanna's initiation required a descent into a feared realm, remote and separate from the upper world of light and life. Inanna's descent into death in the underworld and her ultimate ascent into new life, offers a paradigm that death is an inseparable part of life and not something to be feared.

## Rites of Communion With the Goddess: the Hierogamos

Sexual union of the goddess with her consort or *son-lover* as the person who mated with the goddess was called, occurred in the ritualization of a sacred marriage rite, which symbolized the union of the moon and sun, and of heaven and earth. This sacred marriage rite was later known in Greece as the *hierogamos* and was carefully scheduled to align with the phases of the moon. It was celebrated in the spring with the return of the king from the underworld. The high priest or king of the city enacted the role of the newly risen vegetation god, known during the time of Inanna as Dumuzi, or Tammuz, while a priestess of the temple *became* the goddess Inanna. This ecstatic coupling was seen as the vivifying energy that would ensure the fecundity of the crops, promising fertility and happiness for the entire community. It was the most important ritual for the renewal of fertility of the land because it brought together in sacred sexual union the goddess and the god.

The experience of sexual ecstasy wasn't reserved solely for the gods and goddesses, however. Sacred sexual priestesses serving in the temples to the goddess were trained in the ecstatic arts and could initiate any man who came to the temple for that experience. It was through the power of ritual and ceremony that the priestesses transformed what we might consider today as an ordinary act of sexual intercourse into a spiritual experience, a *rite of communion* with the deity. To serve as a sacred sexual priestess was an honor and the women were sometimes called the "holy virgins," the word *virgin* in pre-Christian times simply meaning that a woman was unmarried and did not denote her sexual status.

## WRITING EXERCISES

1.  Most of us learned in school that writing originated in Sumer around 3,100 BC but it wasn't until the 1920s that a British archaeologist Sir Woolley and his wife were digging at the ancient Sumerian city of Ur, home to the Biblical Abraham, when they uncovered a treasure trove of magnificent artifacts identified as the Royal Tombs of Ur. The breathtaking ceremonial garb they discovered was thought to have been actual artifacts used in the ancient re-enactment of the *Descent Myth of Inanna*, and gives us some idea of the importance of the seasonal ritual drama performed in the courts of the temple complex at Ur. Nothing so far has ever been found in Mesopotamia that compares with the wealth of these tombs and their cultural brilliance.

    Mrs. Woolley was the only woman on the team of excavators but only her husband Woolley and several other American archaeologists were given any credit for discoveries made at the famous dig site.

    >   Imagine yourself on a similar dig site. What do you discover? How do you interpret your findings? If your interpretations are different from your male colleagues, how do you feel and what do you say and do? Do you write papers and go on lectures telling of your findings and contrary interpretations? Do your discoveries help to restore a lost connection to women's ancient past? If so, how are they relevant to women in contemporary society?

2.  One of the most outstanding fines of Woolley's excavations, and for writers, one of the most exciting, was a small alabaster disc showing a woman's figure on one side and an inscription on the back of a woman's name: *Enheduanna*. Enheduanna was an actual historical person, a royal Princess and daughter of the historical King Sargon. Since this discovery, Enheduanna has come to be referred to as the *Shakespeare of the Ancient World* because she wrote countless hymns and poems to honor the Goddess Inanna, becoming the first poet and writer of the ancient world. What was also unusual about Enheduanna was that she not only wrote hymns to Inanna, but amazingly she also wrote about her personal life, detailing how she was in danger because the temples to the Goddess Inanna were being threatened with destruction.

    *Disk of Enheduanna*, University of Pennsylvania Museum of Archaeology and Anthropology, Philadelphia. *Printed here under the Creative Commons CC0 1.0 Universal Public Domain Dedication license.*

    >   Imagine you are Enheduanna, the High Priestess in service to the Goddess Inanna and the first female poet and writer in Sumer. Write a poem or narrative describing yourself, your life and your service to Inanna.

Here is an example of a hymn written by Enheduanna:
> *Lady of all the essences, full of light,*
> *Good woman clothed in radiance*
> *Whom heaven and earth love*
> *You are a flood descending from a mountain,*
> *O primary one,*
> *Moon goddess Inanna of heaven and earth!*

3.  Before setting off on her heroine's journey to visit Enki, the God of Wisdom from whom she intends to steal the symbol of rulership known as the *me* or sacred laws, Inanna prepares herself in a unique way. Instead of brandishing a sword like a male hero in preparation for what will be many physical challenges on his hero's journey, she exalts her vulva in a very proud and straightforward manner. Here are the first few lines of the cuneiform text translated by Samuel Noah Kramer:

> *Inanna placed the shugurra, the crown of the steppe, on her head.*
> *She went to the sheepfold, to the shepherd*
> *She leaned back against the apple tree.*
> *When she leaned against the apple tree, her vulva was wondrous to behold.*
> *Rejoicing at her wondrous vulva, the young woman Inanna applauded herself.*

> Write your response to Inanna's preparation for her quest to capture the sacred laws from the God of Wisdom, of her crowning herself Queen and rejoicing at her wondrous vulva, symbol of her womanhood. Imagine what it might have been like to live during a time when women were boldly self-congratulatory of their own sexuality.

4.  Inanna's story teaches us about the tremendous power that can be gained from risk-taking, applauding and affirming oneself and trusting our instincts, the essence of the Wild Woman archetype. All of these characteristics make Inanna a model for independence, courage, and resourcefulness and ultimately of triumph. Her myth also shows us how the dark, repressed aspects of ourselves can be raised to a conscious level and be used to radically change our behavioral patterns and responses

> Imagine yourself as Inanna descending into the Underworld where you will have to leave something signifying your self-hood and power at each of the seven gates. Name the objects you leave at each gate and what they represent to you.

> Now, imagine yourself having arrived in the Underworld, naked and alone, facing the Queen of Death. She is your dark sister and represents the shadow side of yourself. Describe how you feel when she fastens her "eye of death" on you, brutally judges you and condemns you to death. Reflect on what part of yourself is outworn, ready to be discarded and is ready to die so that you can be reborn. To be reborn, however, you will have to make a sacrifice of some kind. Imagine what you will leave behind or sacrifice.

> After three days in the Underworld, spirits come and sprinkle you with the food and water of life and you are reborn. Although you are still yourself, you are also very different. You feel the joy of rebirth rising up inside you. As you slowly ascend from the Underworld to the earth above, you are now complete and whole. Write about your ascent and how you feel now as a new person.

> Write about any additional insights you've gained about your personal journey of initiation and resurrection as reflected in the powerful death/rebirth myth of Inanna.

 ART EXERCISE

5. *CLOAK OF HONOR & HEROISM.* Imagine that a circle of friends is waiting for you when you return from the Underworld. They greet you with shouts of joy and warm embraces. "This is a special cloak to symbolize your heroism in fulfilling your journey," they tell you as they wrap you in an amazing cloak adorned with symbols of transformation.

Take time to review all that you've written in the above writing exercises regarding the myth of Inanna. Gather your ideas for what a *Cloak of Honor & Heroism* given to you by your friends that symbolizes your transformation looks like. Then, create a cloak, as an actual garment of wearing apparel, or a poem describing the cloak and your journey; or, as a drawing, collage or art piece. Create a ceremony to celebrate all that you've been through on your descent journey of initiation and resurrection and ask a group of your friends to attend. Document this ceremony in a creative way meaningful to you, such as a video, an album of photos and writing, or something else.

# Chapter 7: Wild Flesh and The Myth of Feminine Evil

*Does my sexiness upset you? Does it come as a surprise*
*That I dance like I've got diamonds At the meeting of my thighs?*
~from *Still I Rise* by Maya Angelou

We begin by asking ourselves, what do we mean by "Wild Flesh?" Wild Flesh refers to our instinctual sexual natures before they became civilized, shamed, repressed, and declared "evil." When did women's bodies and sexuality become dirty? How was it that much of the world came to believe that women were the instruments whereby evil or sin entered the world? Who created the *Myth of Feminine Evil* and why is it still hanging around our necks like toxic ballast needing to be discarded.

Let's start by taking a look at how western culture regards sexuality, especially women's sexuality and their right to express themselves as they see fit. We all are inheritors of the *Myth of Feminine Evil* and other equally destructive stories and attitudes that have prevented us from expressing ourselves sexually in positive and healthy ways, resulting in a sexual malaise that engulfs much of the so-called civilized world. One of the most pervasive and debilitating expressions of our sexuality has come to be *routine sex* in which sex is an unfeeling, mechanical performance with the goal being to achieve orgasmic release, often only by the man. To break out of this pattern of routine sex, some seek sexual and emotional fulfillment with multiple partners but more often than not, this quest leads to further disappointment because sex, they find out, can't be isolated from what's happening in the rest of their lives.

If nothing else, the so-called sexual revolution and sexual freedom ushered in by the *flower children* of the 1960s exposed the continued widespread perplexity about sex and the moral issues connected with it. According to author Georg Feuerstein in his book *Sacred Sexuality*, the image of a sexual wasteland, which he says began in the 90s, is an attitude towards sexuality that has continued into present times. Feuerstein thinks people are not merely sexually bewildered but are also curiously lost in a cultural landscape that doesn't seem to be able to sustain us morally or spiritually.

For decades, modern women have pleaded for more intimacy when relating to their partner sexually, an intimacy that extends beyond having an orgasm. To address this issue, countless self-help books have been written on the subject; sex therapists have shown up to help; and we've seen the emergence of an emphasis on the esoteric ideas of Tantra, a sexual form of ancient yoga. We'll look at Tantra, its beliefs and mythology in the next chapter. Even with all this openness addressed in books, lectures, movies, sex therapy, online sex groups, and other sexual freedoms such as open marriage, multiple partners, multiple orgasms, vibrators and a wide variety of sex toys, sexual happiness still hasn't been achieved by the vast majority of people and remains illusive.

In addition, the portrayal of woman-as-sex-object continues unabated, a fact that has recently seen more concerted pushback from large numbers of people in newly emerging groups like the *Me-Too* movement in the United States where more women are speaking out against their male sexual perpetrators. Nevertheless, the sex-slave market, online child pornography, and institutional sexual abuse has become more prevalent than ever and thanks in part to the internet and social media, we are more aware of the continuous abuse and violence being perpetuated on women, young girls and boys. We've become painfully aware of the wide gap between what was envisioned by the sexual revolution of the 60s and what is actually still happening in the bedrooms, boardrooms, and churches of today.

In summary, our relationship with sexuality remains a far cry from any experience that we might call Sacred Sexuality or Wild Ecstatic Flesh. How did this happen and as women seeking to reclaim our Wild Woman instinctual nature, what can we do about it?

## Early Christianity and Alienation from the Physical World

There are many points of entry into the subject of how we came to regard our physical bodies with such negativity and disdain, especially women's bodies. Since we are westerners living in the United States, much of how we have come to regard sexuality can be traced to our Judeo-Christian roots, so we'll start there.

During the period after Christ's death, Christianity and its tenets were being shaped against a very diverse, transitional background of philosophies and enormous social and political change. Attitudes toward women were also undergoing tremendous shifts, as peoples' relationship to the earth and a feminine divine presence took a very different turn. The early Christian church, which included Jews and Hellenists as well as Christians, thought they were living in the last days on earth and that God himself would appear and establish a new order. Along with the idea of an imminent coming, it was believed that final victory over evil, chaos and the Goddess, often referred to in the Bible as the Whore of Babylon, would be accomplished.

No longer did people expect renewal through earth rites and celebration. Earth was no longer their proper home. Now, home was in the heavens somewhere in a promised afterlife. Once people were freed from the encumbrances of a physical body, human spirits would be able to soar to the lofty kingdom of God. This shift from belief in renewal of life in the physical earth with our physical bodies to a desire to leave our physicality behind for a more loftier state somewhere in the heavenly realms, had far-reaching effects, ultimately leading to disgust and rejection of our physical bodies and disregard for the earth.

During this period of shifting priorities and beliefs, a person was instructed to free themselves from nature and from the passions and pleasures of the physical flesh. The physical body was thought to "drag the soul down" making it difficult to remain pure in one's spiritual nature, and that the higher intellect or consciousness could only be achieved by freeing oneself from the fetters of the physical body with its uncontrollable passions. The death and resurrection initiation rituals of the old religious cults belonging to the Great Mother gave way to a "salvation" promised in another world, a heaven far beyond the despicable, chaotic earth.

This alienation from the physical world also developed in the classical philosophies of Plato during the same period, approximately the sixth to the second centuries BC. In Egyptian religion, this alienation from the physical world had occurred even earlier, passing from the goddess-life-renewing cults of the Early Kingdom to the later death-centered religions of the New Kingdom. Like the Egyptians before them, Greek religious philosophers had begun to reject the old gods and goddesses, replacing them with a pre-occupation and honoring of masculine love and intellect. According to Plato, for example, the authentic soul only incarnated as a male!

This perception of the soul's salvation existing as a flight from the body and the earth, with its alienated world view, created a personal experience of reality that expressed itself in a *dualistic doctrine of being.* The desired flight from the physical body and the material earth and how it related to women and the existence of a feminine divine also created lasting conflict among the early Christians, specifically between the Gnostic sects and the more mainstream Christians. This new dualistic doctrine of being as perceived by early Christians and Jews played a central role in widening the gap between the sexes and eventually laid the origin of evil at the doorstep of the woman.

## The Birth of the Myth of Feminine Evil

Early Christianity, born out of the apocalyptic Jewish literature of the time and influenced by the Hellenists, drew on many diverse systems of thought in forming its attitudes and religious doctrines, specifically those regarding women as the source of evil having entered the world. In Jewish apocalyptic and rabbinic literature of the second century before the Christian era, there had developed certain explanations for the origins of evil, and although there were several models for explaining evil in the world, the element of female seduction and seeing woman as the serpent or closely allied with a serpent, prevailed as the primary cause of evil.

Women's bodies and sexuality gradually came to be seen as a fountain of evil and darkness, and the transformative power of ecstasy and sexual bliss such as the ancient Goddess Inanna expressed when she exalted her sexuality and wondrous vulva, had long since been repressed and forgotten. These negative attitudes towards women and sexuality soon found their way into the Biblical tale of Adam and Eve, eventually morphing into what became known as the *Myth of Feminine Evil.* It was against this background of dualities of being and rejection of the physical body that the *Myth of Feminine Evil* was born and took hold in the minds and hearts of humanity where, in spite of revolutions to eradicate its insipidness, its toxic effects have remained.

*The Temptation of Eve,*
19th Century by John Roddam
Spencer Stanhope, Collection
of Fred and Sherry Ross

*The Myth of Feminine Evil* was derived directly from the Fall Myth in the Bible's book of Genesis and has become part of Western humanity's creation story. Tracing some of the forgotten strands of the Fall Myth so firmly rooted in our Western mythical heritage and psyche can help us to more fully understand how it came to be that, still to this day for a vast number of people, the accepted belief is that woman was the instrument whereby evil was released into the world.

Even for those who claim no affinity for a story they consider biased and fabricated at best, there can be no doubt of its long-lasting negative influence on women and men's relationships, and how women have come to be regarded. The myth has also functioned to influence laws and attitudes toward women in societies throughout the world.

## The Jewish Watcher Legends

So where did the Bible's Fall Myth have its genesis? Its roots can be traced to certain early Jewish stories called the *Watcher Legends* recorded in the *Book of Enoch* and the *Book of Jubilees*. The *Book of Enoch* presents the *Watcher Legend* as a dream vision that appeared to Old Testament prophet Enoch. There we read that two hundred "Watchers," referred to as angels or "sons of God," have followed their leader to earth where they rape the human women whom they have been "watching," and have "looked upon with lust."

Extraordinarily, it is not the women who have been "defiled" by this contact but the Watchers, even though they have been dispensing charms and various enchanting cosmetics to the women to beautify themselves. Meantime, another fallen angel has been teaching the men how to make swords and knives.

The women raped by the Watchers give birth to giants who turn against mankind, causing war and destruction to break out on earth.

This chaos is reported to God who sends yet another angel to destroy and purify earth, which he does by causing the Great Flood, in which only Noah and his family survive. Evil spirits from the dying giants continue to inhabit earth, however, and evil persists. As punishment, the women who have had intercourse with the Watchers are doomed to become evil sirens while the Watchers are condemned to an eternal burning hell.

Another account appears in the *Book of Jubilees*, when God sends the angels or Watchers to earth to instruct humankind. Only later do the Watchers mate with the human women who give birth to giants and evil breaks out on earth. In later apocalyptic literature, it is the women, not the fallen angels, who are declared the primary instigators of this evil act of disobedience to God.

These sexually-biased themes from myths such as the Watcher Legends of Jewish apocalyptic literature influenced the later Genesis stories from the Bible and were the source of much of early Christianity's prejudices and teachings regarding women and evil. For Christianity, the Fall Myth became the central explanation for all evil. Although the *Watcher Legends* gave way to the Garden of Eden story as the origin of evil, even in apocalyptic literature, Eve, representing all women, and acting in collaboration with the serpent, was retained as the primary source of evil. Using the Fall Myth of Genesis as indisputable evidence and truth, all manner of persecution, brutality and subjection of women became justifiable. According to the Bible, it was because of Eve's transgression that Jehovah punished women for all time by declaring they should suffer in childbirth; and that henceforth, women would have no rights except those acquired through their fathers, sons or husbands.

It is important to note that it was also in the Fall Myth that for the first time the human sexual drive was also connected with evil. Adam and Eve, the myth says, became aware of themselves sexually when the serpent, ancient symbol for the Great Mother Goddess and her sexual initiation ceremonies, educated them regarding their sexuality. "To know" one another was a term used in Biblical scriptures to denote sexual intercourse. "Knowing" one another or having knowledge of good and evil was thus connected to sex. If the female was the source of this evil, meaning the sexual drive, as she was purported to be, then men were justified in dominating and keeping them subservient in order to protect themselves, an attitude we see still reflected today in violent sex crimes where the female victim is blamed for the injustice done to her rather than the perpetrator.

Early Christianity adopted many of these repressive attitudes toward women into its writings and doctrines. It became the mandate for every Hebrew and Christian to destroy and suppress the worship of any female deity wherever it still existed. One by one the temples dedicated to the worship of a female deity were closed while many were converted into Christian sanctuaries.

Likewise, many of the titles belonging to Isis and other goddesses were co-opted by the Catholic Church and applied to the new goddess Virgin Mary. Statues and images of the Virgin Mary nursing her son Jesus Christ were modeled on the older statues of Isis nursing Horus brought back to Europe from the Crusades by the Knights Templar.

These "new images" of the Virgin Mother and child Jesus were carved and placed in churches throughout Europe, which as noted above, had been built over the remains of ancient cultic sites honoring Isis and other local goddesses.

The Great Mother was pronounced dead and the only female left in Christian scriptures was the fabricated and abstract concept of the *Church as Bride to God the Father*. Only one aspect of the former *virgin*-goddesses, *virgin* in its original context meaning a woman who belonged to herself, was now acceptable for women: the nurturing, life-giving, maternal aspect portrayed in the image of the Virgin Mary, mother to Jesus, whose physical body had never been penetrated by a man. Mary was a "new" kind of virgin; a woman who had never experienced her body sexually. The shadow side of the Great Mother, the wild, dangerous side that contained the uncontrollable passions of the body, were all relegated solely to the realm of the dark underworld, the dangerous chasm, the bowels of the earth, with no possibility of redemption except through the figure of Jesus Christ, who now instead of being her consort or *son-lover* in the sacred marriage ritual celebrated for thousands of years in the ancient Mother Goddess religion, was now her savior.

By identifying the male part of humanity with the divine and associating women with evil or the demonic enabled the belief in *The Myth of Feminine Myth* to continue and has led to the concept of male supremacy both in the divine and human realms. Author and theologian Joan Engelsman says in her book, *The Feminine Dimension of the Divine* that unfortunately half of the dualities that are indicative of the feminine divine are not presently regarded as qualities of God. On the contrary; rage, chaos, darkness and earthiness are usually identified as properties of Satan…(and that) this deep symbolic connection between the feminine and evil cannot be avoided, although they are not identical, they do seem inseparable."

 WRITING EXERCISES:

1.  *THE MYTH OF LILITH.* In discussing the Fall Myth, aka, *The Myth of Feminine Evil,* we would be remiss if we didn't talk about someone else who was there *before* Eve in the Garden of Eden. Her name was Lilith, a name derived from the Sumerian word "lil", meaning wind. Lilith was an early daughter of the Great Goddess whom orthodox Jews feared because she represented the continuing temptations to the cult of the Goddess. In an early Jewish text she is referred to as Lilith, the harlot, the wicked, the false, and the black one. According to some researchers, her "forbidden" mysteries and teachings were the techniques of Kundalini yoga leading to sexual consciousness, all of which brings us to the Adam and Eve story. Hebrew legend says Lilith was created simultaneously with Adam and that they argued over what position to take during sexual intercourse. Rebellious Lilith refused to lie on her back side during intercourse, and unwilling to forego her equality with Adam, flew off into the air away from Eden, speaking as she went the unspeakable name of God. Some legends say she flew to the desert where she had orgies with elemental spirits and sand demons and bore hundreds of demon children every day.

    In the 70s an article appeared in the New York feminist newspaper *Majority Report* that gave a *sisterhood is powerful* version of the Fall Myth. Author Claire Randall called her article *Applesource: The Coming of Lilith* in which she completely revised and re-visioned the Fall Myth. In her humorous account, she details a friendship that develops between Lilith and Eve, which changes the entire story to one of women's empowerment. In the beginning of Randall's story, Eve doesn't know anything about Lilith until one fine day when Lilith returns from her home in the faraway desert and sets herself up outside the Garden of Eden. That's when the two women begin to talk, share many wonderful ideas, laugh and cry together, and eventually become friends, all to the puzzlement of both Adam and God. Randall ends her revised story with, "And God and Adam were expectant and afraid the day Eve and Lilith returned to the garden, bursting with possibilities, ready to rebuild it together."
    >    Write your own version of the Fall Myth that includes the character of Lilith.

2.  Think about a movie you've seen lately, a book you've read or a story you've heard about violence, rape or murder being perpetrated on a woman. Describe how you felt; were you scared, upset, determined to take some positive steps to prevent further violations against women? Do you think our society has grown numb about the violence and abuse committed against women? Do you think public outrage as exhibited in the *Me Too* movement is making a difference in how women are perceived and being treated?

3.  Author Ashley Montague wrote very convincingly in his book *The Natural Superiority of Women* published in 1970 that men have sought dominance and control over women because they were jealous of women's power. Write your thoughts on this idea.

4.   In 1896, early feminist Elizabeth Cady Stanton took much of the wind out of the *Myth of Feminine Evil* when she made the following astute observation. "Take the snake, the fruit-tree and the woman from the tableau and we have no fall, no frowning judge, no inferno, no everlasting punishment, hence no need of a Savior. Thus, the bottom falls out of the whole Christian theology. Here is the reason why in all the Biblical researches and higher criticism, the scholars never touched the position of women."

>   Write your reactions to *The Myth of Feminine Evil*. In what ways do you feel this ancient story still impacts women's lives today and in particular your own? How and what could you and other women and men do to change this myth?

*Severed Headed Vajrayogini,* artist unknown
permission granted by David Lai, www.davidlai.me

# Chapter 8: Sacred Sexuality: A Reverence For All Life

*Each pond with its blazing lilies Is a prayer heard and answered*
*Lavishly, every morning.*
*Whether or not*
*You have ever dared to be happy,*
*Whether or not*
*You have ever dared to pray.*
~from *Morning Poem* by Mary Oliver

Is there such a thing as Sacred Sexuality and if so, what does it mean? By Sacred Sexuality I'm referring to an idea that encompasses much more than positive or pleasurable feelings being exchanged between lovers. Sacred Sexuality is a way of looking at the world in which all aspects of life are considered sacred. When defined in this way, Sacred Sexuality includes not only how we engage with our senses in a personal, sexual way; it includes how we engage with everything around us, from our environment, the trees, animals, oceans, forests, to our families, our next door neighbors, our communities and to our world. In other words, how we engage with all of creation.

Sacred Sexuality is a conscious reverence and re-enchantment of everyday lives and our everyday world. When we experience and embody the bliss of our authentic, everyday being, we get in touch with a reality that includes but far exceeds the pleasurable sensations of the body. This bliss of living inside an orgasmic universe, described by religious mystics as an *ecstasy of spirit*, includes our sexuality as well as the miracle of all life and existence.

We have already traced in some detail how our early ancestors worshipped a Great Mother goddess and how it came to be that temples dedicated to her worship were destroyed and her myths radically altered or repressed. Along with this long process of destruction came the dishonoring of women, and as we saw in the last chapter with *The Myth of Feminine Evil*, eventually women and their bodies were declared the vehicle through which evil entered the world.

How can we restore an attitude of honor, respect and a sense of the sacred to women and how we regard women's bodies? How can we learn to celebrate the joyful expression of an individual's sexuality and sexual choices? How can we restore a sense of the sacred into an expression of our sexuality that includes how we regard and respond to the natural world and all its inhabitants?

To answer these questions, we're going to consider myths of the ancient Greek Goddess of Love and Beauty, Aphrodite, and see what we can learn from her archetype. Then, we'll look at the *Sky Dancers* or *Dakinis* from the Tantric Buddhist tradition and a myth about one of the founding mothers, Laksminkara, that provide entirely new perspectives to many Westerners regarding sexuality and the crucial role women have played and continue to play in bringing forth respect and an equality of the sexes.

## Aphrodite, Greek Goddess of Love

As civilizations changed and developed through the millennia, the Great Mother became associated not only with fertility but also with other aspects of her being. Through the image of the Greek Goddess Aphrodite, known as the Goddess of Love and Passion, the feminine form took on a distinct kind of sensuous beauty. The word *Golden*, connoting radiance and beauty, was the most frequent epitaph used by the Greeks to describe Aphrodite. As a symbol of the transformative and creative power of love, she inspired poets who told of the beauty of her face and graceful form, her golden hair, flashing eyes, soft skin and beautiful breasts. To the ancient Greek poet Homer, Aphrodite was "a lover of laughter, filled with irresistible charm."

*Birth of Aphrodite.* Ludovisi Throne, around 460 BC. Plaster cast. Gallery of Classical Art in Hostinné. Photo credit: Zdenek Kratochvil *Printed here using the Attribution-Share Alike 4.0 International license.*

She was also a favorite subject for the Greek sculptors who portrayed her nude or partially dressed, revealing her graceful, sensual body, seen in the sculptures of Venus de Milo and the Aphrodite of Cnidos, known to us through Roman copies of the originals. Centuries later Aphrodite's sensuality and beauty were portrayed by artist Botticelli in his well-recognized painting *Birth of Venus* in which she is depicted nude, standing on a shell, having arisen out of the ocean mists. Twentieth century pop artist Andy Warhol even created his version of Botticelli's *Birth of Venus* with his repetition of images of her face painted in multiple colors.

In the past, it was through the archetypal image of Aphrodite, the sensuous figure of a goddess of love, that an individual woman could become aware of her own sexual feminine nature. Establishing a right relationship with this goddess archetype, however, became extremely difficult after the patriarchal religion took hold and the goddess, instead of being venerated suffered a loss of reverence and "women came to worship gods made by men; men's values became her values; men's attitudes, justifying the subordination of women, became her attitudes."[1]

According to author and Jungian analyst Nancy Qualls-Corbett, along with the obliteration of the goddess went the concept of woman being "one-in-herself," and now a woman defined herself almost exclusively in terms of her relation to man, often seeing herself as inferior. The results of removing reverence for or worship of a Goddess of Love as seen in the archetype of Aphrodite, consequently meant there was no container for sexual ecstasy.

To restore the multi-faceted image of the feminine archetype to its former vitality and relevancy in women's lives, we must first become aware that the current existing images are inadequate to contain the fullness of this passionate life force because they often only exist in a duality of being: either a nurturing,

---

1    Nancy Qualls-Corbett, *The Sacred Prostitute: Eternal Aspect of the Feminine,* p. 118.

caring Madonna type or a sexually-driven whore or mistress. The point is, that women in their search of the archetypal divine feminine in themselves, must first find *positive* images of the feminine that include the erotic aspects of the goddess as well as the compassionate and nurturing ones.

In the following sections we'll take a closer look at myths of Aphrodite and the Yoginis of Tantric Buddhism that contain both the compassionate face of the feminine as well as the erotic aspects as we consider ways to include them in our lives.

## Why the Goddess of Love Still Matters

Noted author and psychiatrist Jean Shinoda Bolen brought to life the ancient Greek Goddesses to contemporary women in her best-selling book *Goddesses in Every Woman: A New Psychology of Women* by showing women how to identify the various archetypes of the Greek Goddesses in their own lives and how they could learn and grow by familiarizing themselves with their myths. Bolen called Aphrodite an *alchemical goddess* and considered her to be in a category all her own because of the magical process and power of transformation that she alone possessed in Greek mythology; her presence alone was known to cause mortals and deities alike to fall in love and conceive new life.

Myths say Aphrodite was born out of the foam of the ocean and was exquisitely beautiful Throughout all her myths, she had more sexual liaisons than any of the other goddesses and although she wasn't a virgin goddess like the Lady of the Wild Things, Artemis, she was like Artemis in that she did as she pleased and never sought approval from anyone. Like Hera, wife of Zeus, and the Grain Goddess Demeter and her daughter Persephone, Aphrodite was linked with male gods; however, unlike these goddesses, Aphrodite was never victimized nor did she suffer from male abuse. In all her relationships the feelings of desire were mutual and she was never a victim of a man's unwanted passions.

Bolen's insights into modern women who are infused with the Aphrodite archetype are helpful in understanding how to recognize her presence and how to effectively work with those energies.

According to Bolen, a modern woman infused with the Aphrodite archetype values emotional experiences with others more than either independence or permanent bonds to them. While the Aphrodite archetype values relationships, she doesn't seek long-term commitments to others; rather, she seeks to consummate relationships and generate new life. *So, this archetype is expressed through physical, sexual intercourse or through the creative process.*

Further, an Aphrodite woman, according to Bolen, focuses on what is personally meaningful to her and doesn't let others divert her from her goals. What she values is solely subjective and cannot be measured in terms of achievement or recognition by others. Whenever her archetype is present in a woman, for example, her effect isn't limited to the romantic or sexual, however; Platonic love, soul connection, deep friendships and emphatic understanding, which are also expressions of love, can also be present.

Bolen presents three key understandings of this archetype that are helpful to our understanding. If Aphrodite is present as a major archetype in a woman's personality, she falls in love often and easily, which can be a problem in today's culture where sensuality and sexuality in women are often degraded and where a woman who takes many lovers is considered a temptress or worse yet, a whore. Another aspect of Aphrodite women is that they gravitate toward men who are not necessarily good for them or to them and unless other goddesses have an influence, their choice of men goes to those who are creative, complex, moody or emotional—men like the Gods Hephaestus, Aries and Hermes. Such men don't aim for occupational pinnacles or positions of authority and they don't want to be heads of households, husbands or full-time fathers.

A third understanding according to Bolen is that an enduring monogamous marriage is often difficult for an Aphrodite woman. Again, unless other goddess archetypes are influential in containing Aphrodite within the marriage, or the marriage is a particularly fortuitous combination, she'll probably follow a pattern of serial relationships, much like the beautiful and sensuous Hollywood actress Elizabeth Taylor whose public image was that of a contemporary Aphrodite and who had a string of failed marriages.

Bolen says that for the lesbian Aphrodite woman, the only differences between her and her heterosexual counterpart are her sexual preferences because she too becomes intensely involved in relationships, falls in love often and easily and as a consequence usually has a series of important relationships. Wanting to experience everything life has to offer, she may have sexual relationships with men and women. Unconstrained by the need to live up to what men expect women to be, a lesbian Aphrodite, perhaps more than her heterosexual counterpart, exercises Aphrodite's prerogative to pick and choose her lover. The alternative lifestyle that the lesbian community offers suits her lifelong unconventionality.

## Ways To Grow Beyond the Archetype

Bolen's book presents *ways to grow beyond the archetype*. This begins by learning about your own archetypal pattern. For the women who resonant with the Aphrodite archetype, for example, it helps them to know that it is their "goddess-given" nature to fall in love easily, to experience erotic attractions and to have a strong sexual drive that many other women don't have. This knowledge, according to Bolen, helps free Aphrodite women from guilt for being who they are. At the same time, she insists, they must become aware that they must look out for their own best interests, because the goddess will not!

Once a woman becomes conscious of her Aphrodite pattern and decides to modify it, a major shift can occur. Making choices and shaping consequences so that she or others she loves won't be hurt, allows her to sort out her priorities and act on them. For example, in the myth of *Psyche and Eros,* Psyche faces the confusing and seemingly impossible task of sorting through an enormous pile of seeds all jumbled together in a large room. Bolen says that when a woman must make a crucial decision, she often has to first sort out a jumble of conflicting feelings and competing loyalties. This "sorting the seeds" is first and foremost an inward task assigned to her by the Goddess Aphrodite, and requires that a woman look honestly within herself; sift through her feelings, values, and motives in order to separate what is truly important from what is insignificant. By learning to stay with a confusing situation and *not* act until clarity emerges, she learns to trust her own intuitive process, which is an important task of reclaiming the Wild Woman archetype and one's instinctive nature.

 WRITING EXERCISES

1.  The following is a list of *Vows to Aphrodite*. First, read them out loud. Then, take several of the vows that you most identify with and write how they relate to you and your sexuality. You might also want to include them in the art exercise below called *My Creative Life*.

    VOWS TO APHRODITE

    *I accept that I am strong alone and choose relationship only when and as long as it prospers and pleases me. I fulfill myself through my work, my play and my living.*

    *I am a Holy Warrior, a Wise Woman, a Wild Woman, who expresses her spirituality and sexuality through all aspects of my beingness. I joyfully accept the total responsibility for my life and my soul's evolution.*

    *I am exalted and made holy (whole) in the complete expression of my sexuality. I affirm and praise myself as I courageously express my full sexual being.*

    *I am exalted in the expression of my sexual instincts and passions. I am capable of caring and nurturing myself emotionally. Every relationship I enter, regardless of its length of time, is a committed, perfect relationship.*

    *I create and manifest everyone and everything I need and desire to be a Fully Realized being---sexually, spiritually, mentally and emotionally. I am whole (Holy) and complete within myself. I am beholden to no man or woman.*

    *I express myself sexually because it pleases me to do so. Everything, everyone, every situation I create pleasures me. I embrace all Ecstasy. I choose the path to my wholeness of Bliss and Ecstasy.*

    *I release the path of pain, sorrow, regret and suffering. I am wiling to allow any pleasurable relationship to assume its own destiny within my life. I make no effort to control, mold, fix-up or change it.*

    *I trust the rightness of all relationships in my life. I trust myself to be sexually intimate when it pleases and supports me to do so. I trust myself to immediately release any and all relationships that are in any way hurtful or harmful to me.*

    *And so it is, Goddess Aphrodite, whose blessings I seek and accept.*

2.  Gloria Steinem, feminist, journalist and creator of *MS. Magazine*, published a best selling book in 1986 called *Marilyn/Norma Jeane*. Like the Greek Goddess Aphrodite, Hollywood actress Marilyn Monroe was considered a goddess of irresistible sexuality and is still revered today. In her book Steinem reveals the woman behind the myth by looking at the attitudes in America that shaped Monroe into a sexual icon of the Aphrodite archetype.

    >   Imagine you are a journalist for *MS. Magazine* and have been assigned to interview Marilyn Monroe, who is an older woman now and lives a secluded life in upper state New York. Write out the questions you will ask her regarding her image as a sex goddess and how that played out in her life. Then write her responses and your reflections on what she said.

71

## ART EXERCISE

3.   Create an art collage called MY CREATIVE LIFE, using photos, pictures from magazines, cards or drawings you assemble. Use words or quotes to further illustrate what your writing/creative life looks like. Be sure and include what or how a sacred sexuality plays a part in your life.

## MORE WRITING EXERCISES

4.   In Nancy Qualls-Corbett's book *The Sacred Prostitute: Eternal Aspect of the Feminine*, she says that any ancient connection between spirituality and passionate love was lost to the depths of the unconscious when the Goddess of Love was relegated to a low status and disrespected. When the Goddess of Love was still honored, women could embody both the *sacred prostitute and virgin*, as those words were originally intended, and could experience her sexuality with a radiant confidence and sensuality reflecting that of the goddess of love herself.

   >   Write your response to the ideas of a woman being able to contain both aspects of her sexuality as contained in the *sacred prostitute and virgin,* as originally defined. Do you find these ideas relevant to today's woman in assisting her being able to express her sexuality more freely, with passion and self-respect?

   >   How do you see and experience your body? How does your instinctual inner Wild Woman experience her body? Is there a difference? If so, write how they might come together in a fuller, more authentic expression of your sexuality.

5.   What are some of your ideas regarding the title of this chapter, "Sacred Sexuality: A Reverence For All Life?" Write what it means to you in terms of the idea that everything we encounter is sacred.

## Embracing the Possibility of Passionate Enlightenment

To many Westerners, Tantric Buddhism is known primarily for its sexual practices and practitioners who strive to transform erotic passion into spiritual ecstasy. Religious scholar and professor Miranda Shaw has written an award-winning book called *Passionate Enlightenment* that focuses exclusively on the Buddhist women who helped to found the Tantric movement and their creative role in shaping its gender relations and in re-defining a sacred sexuality. Shaw argues that it was an unconscious motivation to preserve the patriarchy that has for so long fueled the denial of women as full-participants in Tantric circles and as co-creators of the Tantric Buddhist tradition.

According to some scholars, Tantric Buddhism was a socially inclusive movement that emerged in India during the Pala period, 8ᵗʰ to 12ᵗʰ centuries that drew on the many diverse elements of Indian culture. Tantra arose outside the intellectual and powerful Buddhist monasteries of monks and nuns as a protest movement by lay people.

The Tantric movement embraced a radical revision of the prevalent values and practices of Buddhism that was, for all intents and purposes, a new religious paradigm. Reformers believed that self-mastery was to be tested in places like the family, the town and the marketplace, as well as cremation grounds where the dead were buried and the dangerous, isolated wilderness areas. Unlike the proponents of early Christianity who sought freedom from the physical body and their passions, the Tantric reformers insisted that desire, passion and ecstasy were to be embraced and that mastery over these desires could only be achieved by *immersion* into them rather than flight from them. This belief allowed sexual intimacy to become a major component of Tantric ritual and meditation.

According to Shaw, the most relevant feature of the new Tantric literature was how women were to be regarded, requiring an absolute attitude of respect and homage as revealed in this quote from a major Tantric scripture of the *yogini-tantra* class:

*One who knows this yoga should always worship,*
*By the method of wisdom and skillful means,*
*Mother, sister, daughter, and niece.*
*He should always worship women*
*With his powerful scepter of wisdom,*
*Even crippled women, artisans, and women of the lowest class.*[2]

Worship of the sacred *yoni,* a woman's vulva, was also present in ancient Tantric Buddhist texts and was seen as being both the gateway to life and the citadel of Buddhahood. Shaw says that the male practitioner was directed to contemplate the womb of his partner in realization that this part of a woman's anatomy was the passageway to his numerous rebirths and now could become a threshold to enlightenment.

A woman didn't need male approval if she wanted to participate or advance in Tantric circles but a man's progress in Tantra was decidedly marked by his relationships with women and his showing the proper regard towards them was a prerequisite to his enlightenment.

The terms *yogini* and *dakini* were used to describe female Tantrics and were titles of honor. *Yogini* was a word meaning a female practitioner of yoga or the ritual arts and indicated someone who might possess magical powers; or she might be an actual deity. The word *dakini* was translated as "sky-walker," "woman who flies," or "female sky-dancer," emphasizing the flights of spiritual insight and ecstasy they embodied as a result of their having realized a state of emptiness or enlightenment.

The Tantric Buddhist tradition embraced a wholistic perspective of life and living, which by definition includes those aspects considered by some to be undesirable. For the Tantricas, enlightenment could be found in all human activities. Advocates of this new breed of Buddhism also insisted on the necessity of embracing emotions such as passion, desire and ecstasy. Similar to the sacred ritual

---

2    Miranda Shaw, p. 40, "Women in Tantric Theory," from *Passionate Enlightenment*

of *hierogamos* of the Great Goddess traditions of the Near East, Tantra taught that the body wisdom obtained through sexual intimacy was a sacred sacrament whereby all who participated obtained the possibility of enlightenment.

## The Myth of Laksminkara & The Severed-Headed Vajrayogini Meditation

The life story of Laksminkara, a founding mother of Tantric Buddhism, describes her journey to seek the ultimate truth leading to enlightenment. Here's the story of Laksminkara as adapted from Miranda Shaw's book *Passionate Enlightenment*.

*Having been born into a royal family, Laksminkara was a princess and lived a life of luxury and privilege in a royal palace. She was well-educated, studied meditation and as a child played with her childhood friends in the beautifully manicured royal palace gardens where peacocks and parrots roamed freely.*

*Her life was idyllic, but all that changed one day when she found out that she had been betrothed to the King of Ceylon. Full of excitement, happy anticipation and carrying a lavish dowry, Laksminkara traveled to Ceylon to meet her fiancé, but her heart sank when he arrived to meet her carrying the skins of deer he had killed, offering them to her as a tribute.*

*Laksminkara knew she couldn't marry a merciless hunter and hid herself in one of the palace's rooms, yelling and throwing things at anyone who tried to approach her. In despair, when night descended upon the palace, she slipped away into the darkness. She tore off all her silk clothing and jewels and rubbed her body with ashes, giving it a tint of blue; then she unbound her perfumed hair that had been braided with jasmine flowers and vowed to never again braid it or tie it back. In spite of her efforts to disguise herself, she was discovered; however, not giving up, she began to talk incoherently, pretending to be mad, an act of deception certain to make herself unmarriageable. Of course, the marriage was immediately cancelled because who would want to marry a mad woman?*

*At last, freed from marriage with a man she vehemently disliked, Laksminkara made her way to a cremation ground, hoping to avoid anyone that might come in search of her. But no one would have recognized her as the former princess. Now, she wore no clothes and her long hair, matted with dirt and leaves, hung down around her body.*

*Laksminkara spent her time in solitude, and was soon able to communicate directly with the Buddhas and bodhisattvas who gave her religious instruction. During this time of seclusion, the female Buddha Vajrayogini appeared to her in a vision. Her long black hair hung loose and her yellow body was angled in a dramatic dancing pose exposing her vulva. Most dramatic of all, however, was Vajrayogini's severed head, which she carried high above her in triumph. Three streams of blood poured from her neck where her head had been severed; one stream flowed into the mouth of her severed head and the other two into the mouths of two yoginis who were at her side. This became the meditation practice that Laksminkara brought forth after she left her seclusion, calling it the Severed-Headed Vajrayogini.*

*For the meditator to engage in the Severed-Headed Vajrayogini practice, Laksminkara encouraged them to find a secluded place to practice and to imitate the deity by wearing her hair loose and "clothed with the sky," or naked. Then the practitioner was to draw a triangle with vermillion or with her own menstrual blood, which would be a place for offerings; again showing the universality of the triangle as an ancient symbol for female creative power. Identifying herself with the deity, the mediator was to envision herself raising a sword and cutting off her own head and waving it aloft in triumph. Cutting off the head signified a release of the ego and a severing of dualistic thinking at its root, which offered a direct way of knowing beyond conceptual dualities. This act also showed that a woman's body could provide sustenance for itself and showed that she had a never-ending stream of energy (blood) within her that she could direct for her own liberation.*

 WRITING EXERCISES:

1.    Write your response to the story of Laksminkara, one of the early mothers of Buddhism. Do you think the "Severed-Headed Vajrayogini" practice she introduced could be beneficial to women today?

2.    Would you consider Laksminkara an archetype that embodies the essence of the Wild Woman and a woman's instinctual nature?

3.    Have you ever considered that you could obtain a higher state of awareness through expression of your sexuality?

4.    Is there a place in your worldview for the consideration or incorporation of a Sacred Feminine in your spiritual practice and beliefs? Do you think it would make a difference in the way women are treated if there were a Mother Goddess, or a Female Divine figure present in the world's religions? Or, do you feel we can just as easily find fulfillment by envisioning ourselves as being part of an orgasmic universe that represents or contains a *Sacred Sexuality of All Beings*?

*White Buffalo Calf Woman,* by Vera Louise Drysdale
*printed here by permission of the artist.*

# Chapter 9: Wild Woman's Passion: Source of Our Creativity

*The meaning of life is creative love. Not love as an inner feeling, as a private sentimental emotion, but love as a dynamic power moving out into the world and doing something original.*
~from *If Aristotle Ran General Motors* by Tom Morris

How can we recover a passion for our creative being and self-expression that is imbued with the power of our instinctual wisdom? One important way is through storytelling and remembering myths that speak to a time when we felt no separation between "us" and "out-there-other." Within the energy of a story, the Wild Woman archetype has survived for millennia, often going undetected or if seen, she was ridiculed as something no longer having any relevancy or importance to our modern-day world. But her wildish essence is still here and we can feel her energy presence everywhere around us, in the wind that blows through our hair like the Yoginis or Sky Dancers whose hair hung loose around their shoulders; or when we engage in our everyday activities with an awareness of the sacredness of ordinary things; when we sit quietly beside a mountain stream and lose ourselves, merging into the oneness of its mesmerizing gurgle, flowing over and under river bed rocks and tree branches; or watching a pair of cooper's hawks flying back and forth with insects in their mouths to feed their young nestlings in the tree tops along the *Acequia Madre* or Mother Ditch when spring comes to New Mexico; breathing in deeply the distinct, delicious smell of pinion wood burning in the northern New Mexico fireplaces and wood stoves in the winter-time cold; or any experience that takes us inward.

We only have to pause, listen and pay attention to the countless ways Wild Woman still presents herself to us. To date, I've not personally seen or felt her on social media, video games, or virtual reality.[1] She is Wild Woman and by definition must be found in the wild places in nature, in our dreams, in the passionate expression of our creativity, our sexuality and in our inner psyches where she lives as an archetype.

In this chapter, we'll look at myths that embody the Wild Woman archetype, selected because they have something special to teach us about our relationship to our own creativity and passion. First, there is the story of *La Loba* from the desert lands of the United States as told by the Hispanic people; followed by the story of *White Buffalo Calf Woman* from the Lakota Sioux tribe of Native America; and finally, from across the ocean and the Celtic Islands, the *Myth of Ragnell, Celtic Goddess of Sovereignty*.

---

1     We will look at the role technology is playing in shaping us and our world in Chapter 11.

## The Myth of La Loba, the Bone Collector

Like any artist and collector of unusual objects found in nature, from ocean shells to rocks in a mountain stream, or bones from the desert, the story of *La Loba* or Wolf Woman is about an old woman who collects bones from the desert places. While La Loba doesn't paint pictures of the desert landscape like the famous visual artist Georgia O'Keeffe did, she does something equally extraordinary; something that can help a woman to get back in touch with her instinctual, wildish senses. Here is La Loba's story as adapted from Clarisse Pinkola-Este's book *Women Who Run With Wolves*.

*The sole work of La Loba is to collect the bones of dead animals and bring them back to life by singing over them. Her cave is filled with the bones of all manner of desert creatures; deer, rattlesnake and crow. But her specialty is said to be the wolf.*

*She creeps and crawls and sifts through the mountains and arroyos looking for wolf bones and when she has assembled an entire skeleton, she sits by the fire and thinks about what song she will sing. When she is ready, she raises her arms over the skeleton and begins to sing, and as she sings the rib bones and leg bones of the wolf begin to flesh out and slowly the creature becomes furred. As La Loba continues to sing, more of the creature comes into being; its ears, nose and finally its tail, which curls upward, shaggy and strong.*

*The wolf creature begins to breathe. Still, La Loba continues to sing, her voice making sounds so deep that the very floor of the desert shakes. Suddenly the wolf opens its eyes, leaps up and runs away down the canyon.*

*Somewhere in its running, whether by the speed of its running or by splashing its way into a river, or by way of a ray of sunlight or moonlight shining directly into its eyes, the wolf is transformed into a laughing woman who runs free toward the horizon.*

 ## WRITING EXERCISES

1. We all begin like a bundle of bones, lost somewhere in a desert, a dismantled skeleton that lies buried under the sand. It is our work to recover the bones, a painstaking process but one we can enlist the help of La Loba as our guide.

   > Write or reflect on your response to these questions: "What are the buried bones of my life and where do I begin to look to find them?" "What in my life is in need of restoration?"

2.  La Loba creates new life from nothing more than the bleached out bones she finds scattered in the desert; then, patiently and with complete authority, she sings her creation song over the bones, bringing them back to life. To sing over our bundle of bones is to breathe over the thing that is ailing us or the thing in us that is in need of restoration. Finding our scattered bones and singing our creation song over them is our work to be carried out in the desert terrain of our psyche.

    > Do you sometimes feel you are nothing more than a collection of bleached out bones scattered about on a desert landscape? Write a creation song or poem to sing over your collected bones to bring them back to life. Then, imagine a ceremony in which you sing your creation song over your collected bones and describe what happens.

3.  Stories are powerful magic. They can even be seen as good medicine. Author Barry Lopez had this to say about stories in his book *Crow and Weasel*: "I would ask you to remember only this one thing," said Badger. The stories people tell have a way of taking care of them. If stories come to you, care for them. And learn to give them away where they are needed. Sometimes a person needs a story more than food to stay alive. That is why we put these stories in each other's memory. This is how people care for themselves. One day you will be good storytellers. Never forget these obligations."

    > Write about any fears you may have regarding your writing and sharing of your stories. Can you think of how people might benefit from hearing your stories?

## White Buffalo Calf Woman, Culture Bringer

*From the endless great prairie grasslands of this ancient continent, the eternal beliefs still whisper to all who see, hear and feel with the heart.* ~Vera Drysdale, *The Gift of the Sacred Pipe*

In the mid 80s, a small number of people, including myself, were part of a uniquely named spiritual group called the *Banana Clan* that regularly gathered to do ritual in a large kiva outside Santa Fe, NM. With our mentor and teacher Robert Boissiere, a Frenchman who had lived several years on the Hopi Indian Reservation and become an adopted member of a family from Second Mesa, our group had made numerous trips to Hopi. In early March of one year, our group decided to make a journey to Hopi to see the Bean dance, part of the Hopi's annual cycle of sacred dance ceremonies performed throughout the year. Even though the snow was piled deep on the ground and the temperatures were well below freezing at the remote region where the Hopi tribe is located in northern Arizona, the ritual of planting bean sprouts in their kivas was seen as an act of faith that the Great Creator would bless their planting of beans, corn and squash in the spring and ensure an abundant harvest in late summer, reminding me of the ancient goddess-worshipping cultures that also marked the cycles of the seasons by planting something in the winter months to symbolize their faith that the Great Mother would bless them with an abundant harvest later in the year.

Among the small group making the trip to Hopi was a lovely older woman, well-known Santa Fe artist Vera Louise Drysdale whose art was shown locally in a prestigious gallery on Canyon Road. Vera painted western landscapes and portraits of Native Americans in scenes from their traditional way of life. Over the next few days she and I were to become good friends.

Vera had just finished writing the Sioux Indian's story of White Buffalo Calf Woman, consulting with Plains Indian's scholar Joseph Epes Brown. In addition to writing the text for the book they would call *The Gift of the Sacred Pipe*, Vera had created eight stunning full color paintings and twenty-eight charcoal drawings for what was to be an illustrated edition of the famous medicine man Black Elk's account of the seven sacred rites of the Oglala Sioux. Vera's art portrayed the arrival of White Buffalo Calf Woman to the Plains Indians and the ancient rituals she gave them, including the sacred pipe, which was to become the central focus in the holy rites of the Sioux.

Over many warm bowls of Indian mutton stew in the restaurant at the Hopi Cultural Center where we were staying, Vera told me of the numerous trips she had made over the years to see Joseph Epes Brown, a Professor at the University of Montana to make sure she didn't stray too far from his version of the rituals as given to him orally, via an interpreter, by the famous Sioux medicine man, Black Elk. In 1953, Brown had published Black Elk's account in a book called *The Sacred Pipe*, but wanted to issue another book containing illustrations. "Brown was difficult to work with," Vera told me with a seriousness that belied her twinkling blue eyes and gentle facial features. "At times, I felt I would be so relieved once our collaboration for the book was over. I've been at this thing for five years." The results of her years of hard work would be a beautiful book that included a condensed version of the rituals as well as her breath-taking illustrations and paintings. Her careful research into the details of ceremonial artifacts as well as daily life brought Brown's text of Black Elk's words to life through her art.

It was the same flawless and detailed research that Vera brought to all of her paintings of Native Americans, which I would find out later in a very profound and personal way. She told me that every summer for many years she and her husband Alex had taken their R.V. and traveled to Indian Pow-Wows of the Plains Indians.

She told me of the deep connection she felt with all the tribes, especially the Sioux. Before we left Hopi, she invited me to visit her studio in Santa Fe.

A few weeks later I drove down from my home in Taos to visit Vera. "Come in," she greeted me with her impish smile. In fact, Vera's last books before she died of cancer a few years later focused on the fairy realms and beings that lived inside rocks and mountain faces. I was quite unprepared that day in her studio for the impact her paintings would have on me.

"Take a look," Vera encouraged as she guided me around her studio, pointing to the numerous paintings of Native Americans that filled the walls of her entire immaculate space. As I began to make my way from one painting to another and then another of the most noble-looking Indian people I had ever seen, I unexpectedly began to cry. Vera had captured the essence of an ancient people whose countenance and prideful bearing communicated an intelligence and sensitivity rarely seen. I had recently worked as a music teacher for the All Indian High School, a boarding school for Native Americans in Albuquerque and knew first hand the struggle native peoples were experiencing as they sought to hold on to their heritage and sacred traditions while also understanding that to succeed in the modern world they would have to walk in many worlds, including that of the white man.

Vera had painted Native Americans as they had been before the invasions of the white man had all but destroyed their culture and ritual ceremonies. Her artistic abilities and sensitivity to the people she painted along with her own vision of the truth of their lives, distinguished her work far beyond a romanticizing of "the noble savage" as painted by earlier artists of the late 19th and early 20th centuries. It was as though she had touched the collective soul of the Indian people, which was reflected in her artistic portrayals of them.

Vera and I became good friends while I lived in the Southwest and I often visited in her Santa Fe studio. During one visit she showed me a recent painting called *Rainbow Warrior*, created specifically for the worldwide celebration called Harmonic Convergence that occurred in 1987. As we sat sipping tea, she revealed personal information to me that she had received through a popular channel called the Tibetan.

"The Tibetan told me that I was the Indian Crazy Horse in a past life, which explains how I have instinctively such detailed knowledge of the Indian way of life, especially of the Sioux."

Vera spoke of the tragic details of Crazy Horses' life and of the death of his young daughter. "She didn't die of cholera as most scholars assumed," she told me. "She died of starvation and the cold weather." As she spoke, she took on the demeanor and tone of what I could only assume was that of Crazy Horse speaking through her. In a painful, deep voice, she told of how the white soldiers had always kept the Sioux on the run, "relentlessly hunting us down so that we didn't have any time to hunt to feed ourselves. Soon the people had no food and began to die. My wife and child died of starvation," she said somberly. "I believe that you Marjorie were that child," she said, turning to me with complete seriousness.

I was stunned and didn't know what to say, having learned the hard way to maintain a healthy dose of skepticism regarding channels, spiritual intuitives or gurus during my years of seeking outside myself for spiritual wisdom and guidance. Vera's reciting of the story of the tragic death of Crazy Horse's child was so real to her that for a few moments I let myself believe what she said. Maybe she had been Crazy Horse, I thought. Maybe I had been his/her child. At the very least, I felt honored that one so close in spirit and knowledge of the Sioux Indians, one who was such an amazing painter and author, one who had led such an incredible life having been born and raised in China to missionary parents…that this one of such stature and talent would single me out as having been the precious child of such a notable leader of the Indians, well, I was honored and I told her so. Otherwise, remaining the skeptic, all I could think was, so this explains why I hate the damn cold weather and snow so much! This very dubious, if not disrespectful, attitude had saved my butt on many an occasion from following home the assorted Pied Pipers who populated the spiritual seekers of the 80s and 90s.

Vera died of breast cancer shortly after I moved to Maui in 1988 and all her artwork was donated to the Akta Lakota Museum & Cultural Center in South Dakota. Although we had often talked of making another trip to Hopi together, we unfortunately never did. While I don't remember much about the Bean dance at Hopi except the bitter cold, Vera and I had become close friends and I was very sad when she passed. During the days and months that followed, I often re-read the ritual brought by White Buffalo Calf Woman to the Sioux Indians, *Keeping of the Soul* from Vera's book, *The Gift of the Sacred Pipe,* whispering to her spirit, "Be at peace Vera Crazy Horse. Be at peace."

## White Buffalo Calf Woman

Here is the story of White Buffalo Calf Woman, which I adapted from *The Gift of the Sacred Pipe* as edited and illustrated by Vera Louise Drysdale.

*Early one morning many winters ago, two Lakota braves were out hunting when they saw someone approaching them in a very wonderful manner. As the mysterious being drew closer, they saw it was a very beautiful woman, dressed in white buckskin and carrying a bundle in her arms. One of the hunters had bad intentions towards the beautiful woman and told his friend about his desires. The second brave was quick to tell him, you shouldn't have such feelings, because she is surely "wakan," a holy woman.*

*As the holy woman drew closer, she motioned for the brave with bad intentions to come over to her. As he did so, a thick cloud quickly surrounded them and when it lifted the sacred woman was standing alone. Lying at her feet, however, was a pile of bones, all that remained of the man who had had bad thoughts towards her.*

*"I have come to your people and wish to talk with your chief," she told the hunter who had recognized her as a holy woman. "Tell him to prepare a large tipi and gather all the people together for I wish to tell them something of great importance."*

*The young brave hastily went to his chief and told him all that had happened and how the sacred woman wanted a lodge constructed and for all the people to gather together inside.*

*Once the lodge was completed, the holy woman came into the camp, and as she walked she sang a song:*

*With visible breath I am walking*
*This nation, the buffalo nation I walk toward*
*And my voice is heard I am walking*
*With visible breath I am walking*
*This scarlet relic For it I am walking*

*She went inside the tipi, carefully holding her scarlet bundle with the sacred relic wrapped inside. "This is a sacred bundle and no one who is impure should ever be allowed to see it," she said to the people. "Inside is a sacred pipe that during the winters to come you will use to send your voices to Great Spirit."*

*The wakan woman took the pipe from the bundle and explained what each part represented. "Every dawn is a holy day," she told them, "because all the light that we see comes from your Father Wakan-Tanka." She told them that they should always remember that the two-leggeds and all the other peoples who walk on the earth are sacred and should be treated in that manner.*

*"Before I leave," she told them, "I want to give you the seven rites of the pipe that you will use." She then gave them instructions for the seven rites which were: Keeping of the Soul; the Rite of Purification;*

*Vision Quest and Crying for a Vision; the Sun Dance; the Making of Relatives; Preparation for Womanhood;*
*and the Throwing of the Ball, which symbolized the earth and gave strength to future generations.*

*As she left the lodge, she turned to the people and said, "Remember how sacred the pipe is and that inside*
*me there are four ages and I will look on you during each age and at the end of the fourth, I shall return."*

*She had walked only a short distance, when the people were amazed to see that she had changed into a*
*young brown buffalo calf. The brown calf walked a little further before it changed into a white buffalo; finally*
*it rolled over on the ground and after bowing to each of the four directions, disappeared over the hill.*

 ## WRITING EXERCISES

1.  There are numerous similarities between the two female characters in the stories of *La Loba* and *White Buffalo Calf Woman*. Like La Loba, White Buffalo Calf Woman sings a song of creation. Like La Loba who sings over the bones she has collected in the desert to give them life, so does White Buffalo Calf Woman breathe her "visible breath" onto the land as she approaches the Lakota people, renewing them and bringing the pipe and traditions that would sustain them and become their spiritual legacy. Both women are also shape-shifters, indicating that they are magical women, shamen and sacred women.

    > To the Lakota people, the life breath in the universe was called *Wakan-Tanka*. Write your thoughts about what "visible breath" means to you in this context. If you are a meditator or yoga practitioner, how does breath affect your practice and understanding of yourself and the world?

2.  We are interested in understanding these two archetypes in order to deepen our passion and commitment to expressing our own creativity and how we might be culture-bearers in our own right.

    > How do you "send your voice" out into the Universe? Do you have special rituals or actions you perform that provide you with a way to connect with what many call a "higher power," or, to Native Americans, a Great Spirit?

## The Myth of Ragnell, Celtic Goddess of Sovereignty

Much of the classic retellings of the myths of the ancient Celts and the roots of Ireland's literary tradition in particular, owe their preservation to a woman named Isabella Augusta Persse born in 1852 in County Galway, Ireland. In 1880, she married Sir William Gregory and was known thereafter as Lady Gregory. She was a central figure in the Irish literary revival after the publication of her book *Irish Myths and Legends*, written after extensive research of Gaelic and countless other manuscripts of Irish myths. Her work inspired a generation of writers, among them Nobel Prize winner and poet William Butler Yeats who based much of his writing on her "reclaimed" stories.

The third myth we'll look at is of Celtic origin, *The Myth of Ragnell*. I first came across this story in a book called *Ladies of the Lake*, written by Caitlin and John Matthews, which portrayed nine of the prominent women in the King Arthur legends. Caitlin Matthews and her husband John have written over 40 books and are experts on the Arthurian and ancient Celtic world. I was fortunate enough to have had a personal exchange with author Caitlin Matthews when she gave a reading of the book at the Ark bookstore in Santa Fe.

Here is Dame Ragnell's story, *The Myth of Ragnell*. as adapted from Matthews' book *Ladies of the Lake.*

*One day while King Arthur is hunting in Inglewood forest, he shoots and kills a stag. Suddenly, out of nowhere a man appears, fully armed and threatens to kill Arthur. The man is Gromer Somer Jour and his grievance is that Arthur has given his lands to Sir Gawain, a knight of the Round Table. He says he will spare the King's life on one condition: that the king return in one year's time to the same spot with the answer to the question: What is it that women love best?*

*Arthur returns to his castle and for months on end worries and ponders what to do. He finally tells Gawain what has happened in the forest and they decide to ride out through the countryside, asking every woman they meet, whether of high or low status, for their answer to the question. Some of the women say the answer is "women want to be well-dressed;" others say "women want to be flattered," while still others are adamant that "women want nothing more than to be loved by a lusty man."*

*The two men return to court with enough answers to fill a large book. But Arthur remains uneasy about the answers he has gotten and decides to go for a ride to clear his head. While out riding, he sees in the distance a lady riding a handsome horse but as she gets closer, he sees that she is indeed a most hideous person in her demeanor, so hideous in fact, that "no tongue could possibly describe her." She tells Arthur that the answers he's been given are useless and that he will certainly lose his life unless he puts his life in her hands.*

*Arthur is amazed and suspicious at the woman's request. She tells him that if he does what she asks, she will give him the right answer to the question he will need when he meets up again with Gromer Somer Jour.*

*The boon she asks is that she will be given to Gawain in marriage. Arthur is astounded, of course, and tells her that he can't possibly agree to her request without asking Gawain himself.*

*Arthur returns to court where he is hesitant to tell Gawain what has happened, but eventually decides he has to tell him of his encounter with the hideous hag who identified herself as Dame Ragnell, and of her offer to save Arthur. Without hesitation, Gawain agrees, assuring Arthur that he would marry the hag twice over if it meant that Arthur's life would be saved. Arthur praises Gawain for his chivalry and returns to the forest to meet Gromer Somer Jour. On the way, he again meets Dame Ragnell and tells her that Gawain has agreed to marry her if she provides Arthur with the correct answer to the question, "What does a woman most want?" Satisfied, Ragnell tells Arthur that the right answer to what every woman wants most is to have sovereignty over her own life.*

*Soon Arthur meets up with Gromer who is waiting in the appointed forest place. First, Arthur shows him the two books full of answers he's gathered, but Gromer dismisses them immediately. Then the king tells him Ragnell's answer and in a rage Gromer admits that it is correct. He curses his sister, who, he says is the only possible woman who could have known the correct answer.*

*On his way back to court Arthur meets Ragnell once again who refuses to leave his side until they have arrived back at the castle and Gawain pledges that he will marry her, a hideous hag.*

*When the day of the wedding arrives, Gawain is somber as he goes to meet his appointed bride. Ragnell is dressed in a lavish white gown but nothing can hide her loathsome and misshapen appearance. Later, at the banquet her table manners are appalling and when the couple retire to the marriage chamber, Ragnell demands that Gawain perform his husbandly duties. As he approaches her, he is stunned at what he sees. Ragnell has turned into a beautiful woman! Gawain doesn't know what to make of the person who was once a hag but is now a ravishing beauty.*

*Gawain asks her who she is and Ragnell replies that she is his wife. There is one thing you must decide, she tells him. You may have me fair either by night or by day, but not both. Gawain agonizes over the choice he must make, but finally tells Ragnell that the choice is hers alone to make. Delighted, Ragnell tells him that by giving her sovereignty, he has broken the spell put upon her and her brother Gromer by a wicked stepmother. From now on she will always be fair.*

*The next morning when Arthur knocks on the door of the newly married couple, he is full of fear that Ragnell may have killed Gawain. But when Gawain opens the door, standing beside him is his beautiful wife, her radiant red-gold hair adorning her beautiful face.*
*Ragnell asks Arthur to forgive her brother Gromer, which he agrees to do.*

*Gawain and Ragnell live happily together and have one son; however, the Sovereign Ragnell only lives but five years after and was much mourned by her husband when she died.*

*Many suspect that Ragnell was no ordinary mortal woman enchanted by her stepmother but was a creature of the Faery Folk, which explains how she was able to change herself from hideous to beautiful.*

 WRITING EXERCISES

1.  For millennia women have had to fight for their *sovereign rights* as we've seen in some detail in preceding chapters. In Matthew's book *Ladies of the Lake* several versions of the Sovereignty myth are referenced, all highlighting a hag who, once she is accepted for who she is, reveals herself as a beautiful woman.

    > Have you experienced having to fight for your *sovereign rights* in your life?

2.  Have you ever joined with other women to fight for your equal rights?

    > Have you experienced judgment for how you look or dress? Describe an especially meaningful situation that happened as a result of how you look or how you dress and what you did or didn't do. Did you have any allies? Have you been the instigator of misjudging other women? What were the circumstances?

3.  The Gaelic story of Ragnell tells of an enchanted woman who must trust a man in order for the spell cast on her to be broken. In this story, she must trust Gawain, a Knight of King Arthur's Round Table, to give the right answer to the question concerning a woman's greatest desire. What makes this story so relevant to our times is that then, as now, freedom has to be accorded to all women and men if there is to be a harmonious balance in the kingdom and the land. Every woman must also afford this to every other woman, something that is often absent today when we see women doing things to undermine and hurt other women. True freedom for women means that the competitive attitude towards other women and men must be dropped. This also includes women dropping their efforts to be more powerful than men, or as feminist-activist Starhawk has named it, "power-over" rather than "power-with" others.

    > Do you feel society, and more specifically, the men in your life demonstrate an understanding that a woman's greatest desire is to have sovereignty over her life and to be accepted exactly as she is?

    > Do you feel any connection to the archetype of sovereignty revealed through the character of Ragnell? Does it matter that she is from the Faery realm?

    > Re-write a modern-day sovereignty myth with characters that carry the same storyline. Does your story differ from the original; if so, how and why?

    > What does Ragnell's question of a woman's sovereignty have to do with restoring a passion to our creative lives?

# Chapter 10: Wild Woman's Relationship to Nature and Art

*If the desert were a woman, I know well what she would be: deep-breasted, broad in the hips, tawny, with tawny hair—eyes sane and steady as the polished jewel of her skies, such a countenance as should make men serve without desiring her passionate, but not necessitous, patient and you could not move her, no, not if you had all the earth to give, so much as one tawny hair's breadth beyond her own desires.*
~from *Lost Borders by* Mary Austin

According to contemporary art critic Lucy Lippard, art and peoples' spiritual experiences were once inseparable aspects of the collective life of prehistoric cultures. Because we won't ever be able to know for certain what ancient sites, art images and artifacts from the past meant to people from those times, Lippard believes that the artistic images and artifacts they left behind can function as aids to our collective memory, functioning like outlets for the imagination that can't be controlled or manipulated like she feels so much of contemporary art attempts to do. "Unlike a towering skyscraper," she says, "a towering standing stone in the landscape seems not so much to dominate its surroundings as to coexist sensuously with them. It confirms the human need to touch, to hold and to make, in relationship to natural forces and phenomena and something seems to flow back to us through these places, which we see perhaps as symbols of lost symbols."[1]

Lippard regards any speculation about the close relationship that existed in prehistory between nature and culture as not some starry-eyed idealization or ahistorical fantasizing about a Golden Age; rather, she makes the case that obviously our ancient kin had a different relationship with nature and the land than we do but that "the reestablishment of a coherent relationship between nature and culture is a critical element in any progressive view of the future." She is quick to point out that the identification of woman with nature and man with culture has, in her opinion, had a damaging effect on women in patriarchal societies where women are regarded as inferior and nature is simply a resource.

"Is there a difference in women artists and male artists?" is an interesting question that Lippard says she no longer asks after having studied thousands of works by female artists early in her career as an art critic. "I could no longer deny," she writes, "that there is a uniquely female expression, although whether this is innate or the result of social conditioning is still a controversial question. Either way, women's social, biological and political experiences are different from those of men; art is born of those experiences and must be faithful to them to be authentic. Therefore, to deny the fact of a woman's art is to neutralize and falsify what women are learning from our new approach to history: that one of the roles of female culture has always been to reach out and integrate art and life, idea and sensation...or nature and culture."[2]

---

1    Lucy Lippard, *Overlay: Contemporary Art and The Art of Prehistory,* p. 8.
2    Ibid, page 42

Lippard believes that the study of prehistoric matriarchal cultures has had a profound influence on contemporary women artists, from the imagery and myths of our ancient female ancestors to the obvious deep connection that existed between women and nature. This is due in part, according to Lippard, to the convergence of feminism and contemporary artists' interest in the culture and art of our ancestors, often labeled "primitivism."

## Frida Kahlo, Artist

The imagery of pre-historical life and nature has been surfacing in contemporary women's art and much of it, according to Lippard, is filled with an anxiety, anger, sexuality and pain. Nowhere is this more apparent than in Mexican artist Frida Kahlo's paintings that are emotional, full of pain and elicit a visceral response from the viewer. This longing for connection to some anthropomorphized Earth Mother, for example, can be seen in Kahlo's painting *Roots (1943)*, which is a self-portrait showing her reclining on a barren plain with stemmed plants or vines growing from a cavity in her chest. A network of red capillaries extending from the leaves, bleed back into the earth while binding her to it.

Another of Kahlo's most vulnerable paintings is called *My Nurse and I* (1937) in which she suckles at the breast of her dark Indian nurse. The baby has the adult head of Frida and the nurse's head is covered with a dark pre-Columbian mask, similar to the famous sculpture of the Aztec goddess Tiazoltcolt in the act of childbirth. Hayden Herrera, Kahlo's biographer, wrote that this painting has Christian overtones,

*Frida Kahlo*, gelatin silver print, 15.2 by 10.8 cm, by Guillermo Kahlo

which he likened to the pain the Virgin felt while suckling the Christ child, knowing of his ultimate crucifixion. In Kahlo's painting the wet nurse doesn't embrace or cuddle Frida. Instead she peers out from behind her black funerary mask, with an open mouth in what Herrera says is a stylized scream. He says that in this painting, Frida transformed the stereotypical mother and child image into one of loss and separation. But Frida does show an inter-connected relationship between nature and human beings when she painted a large leaf in the painting's background of jungle foliage, showing it with engorged, milk-white veins like those of the lactating nurse. In the foliage, there's a praying mantis and a caterpillar metamorphosing into a butterfly, having been nourished by milk from the leaves, just as Frida is being nourished from her nurse's plantlike breast.

 WRITING EXERCISES

1.  *Frida Kahlo*: Since her death in 1954, Frida's life has become something of a myth, making her into a cult figure. Her images are on everything from refrigerator magnets to grocery bags. In Mexico she is hailed as their greatest female artist, and for women everywhere, especially artists, she is an example of great strength, talent and perseverance. During her many surgeries and time in hospitals, and in spite of enormous pain, she painted through it all, with easel propped up in front of her while she lay supine in bed. Her paintings are personal, with many being vivid self-portraits. Initially her work didn't get much attention but that changed when the famous Surrealist painter, Frenchman Andre Breton, met her in Mexico. He was impressed with her work, declaring that she was a Surrealist even though she had no prior knowledge of that style of painting. With his endorsement, she was invited to show her work in a New York gallery. After her well-received show in New York, she traveled to Paris where Marcel Duchamp and Breton, presented her work in a show called "Mexique." She wrote to a friend that she had received congratulations from such famous painters as Joan Miro, Kandinsky, and Picasso. The Louvre bought one of her pieces, a small self-portrait called *The Frame*.

    Frida's paintings from the period when she and her famous muralist husband Diego Rivera were getting a divorce were no longer charming and folkloric, but had become full of anger and rage. In her work *The Two Fridas*, she painted two images of herself, showing the split identity and loneliness she felt at being separated from Diego. One of the Fridas, she told a friend, is the woman that Rivera had loved and the other one dressed in a white wedding dress represented the Frida whom he no longer loved.

    > Whether you are an artist or writer, famous or not, can you identify with some of the challenges Frida experienced as a woman struggling to express herself creatively?

    > Based on your knowledge of Frida Kahlo's life, whether extensive or what you've only heard of her mythic story, do you regard her as a role model to women because she was a woman who experienced success and recognition in spite of her physical limitations and a difficult marriage?

    > Do you agree with art critic Lippard that women's art is often full of pain, anger and anxiety? Do you think art can be a way to heal painful emotions and experiences? What has been your experience with making art as a means to identify and express whatever emotions or feelings you carry inside yourself?

2.  Write about a time when you were infused with passion and inspiration after being in nature. Were you inspired to write, sing, draw, play games, make love?

3.  How important do you think women's art is in helping to re-connect and establish a more intimate relationship to nature?

4.   Do you agree that there is a difference between women's art and that of men? If so, what would you attribute that difference? What do you think of the fact that throughout the centuries women have been compared to nature and men to culture, and the ideas from eco-feminism that say the de-valuation of both women and nature are intertwined?

## Artist as Shaman and Healer

Much has been written about the devastation and destruction that humankind is wielding against the earth, its environment and inhabitants. Thomas Berry, who has been described as a new breed of eco-theologians, has written numerous essays and books that call for a new relationship between humans and the earth in order to recover our connection to the life-sustaining mystery of the earth and its creative energy. He writes, "We are the termination, not the fulfillment of the earth process. If there were a parliament of creatures, its first decision might well be to vote the humans out of the community, too deadly a presence to tolerate any further. We are the affliction of the world, its demonic presence. We are the violation of earth's most sacred aspects."[3]

But where and how does art fit into making or re-making a lost connection to the earth, nature and the landscape where we live? And does it ignite, intensify or affirm the archetype of the Wild Woman? To answer these questions, we'll take a look at a few women who are actively making this healing and creative connection to nature with their art making and with their creative wildish natures in full view.

Having worked as a Fine Art Consultant in an art gallery on Maui for a number of years, I was very intrigued by a book called *The Re-Enchantment of Art* written by art critic Suzi Gablik whose ideas regarding art and its place in our culture as a defining force were, at first, very shocking. Here's what she said was the problem with art and artists today: "In the past we have made much of the idea of art as a mirror (reflecting the times); we have had art as a hammer (social protest); we have had art as furniture (something to hang on the walls); and we have had art as a search for the self." There's another kind of art, however, that exists beyond the "old art-and-life, subject-object polarities to be found in a post-Cartesian framework," which Gablik describes as one that speaks to the power of connectedness; an art that establishes bonds; art that calls us into relationship.

---

3    Thomas Berry, *Creative Energy: Bearing Witness for the Earth*, p. 68.

## Art: Part of A Mythic Crisis?

Gablik believes that in our modern society, most artists are caught up in the cultural myth of aesthetic freedom, and see themselves as "quintessential free agents pursuing their own ends." She also says that our current cultural myths support economic advancement and the autonomous individual rather than myths that embrace ideas of service, compassionate attitudes and communal participation. While she acknowledges that some artists like Wyoming artist Lynne Hull who uses her art to make connections with the land and the animals that live there, most artists haven't made any such shift in their thinking and for them "art remains a question of radical autonomy." According to Gablik, for a long time our society has defined success as money and power so that new ideas or mythologies that seek to redefine personal fulfillment on non-materialistic grounds go right to the core of our culture's "mythic crisis" as regards our art and art makers.

Gablik makes the case that our *cultural coding*, a term she borrowed from theologian Thomas Berry who uses it to describe our cultural traditions, is transferred to us by our mythologies. She says that the cultural coding of modern Western civilization has made its primary focus the ideas of dominance and mastery, giving as examples the dominance of humans over nature, of the masculine over the feminine and the wealthy and powerful over the poor, and so on. She considers it even more alarming that art is included in these current mythologies of domination and mastery and insists that the institutional structures and practices that the art world is modeled on are the same configurations of power and profit that keep the ball of patriarchal capitalism rolling.

Her solution? We have to make a systems shift, create new "ground rules" for our future that aren't situated inside "consumerist imperatives" where art has become something to fill galleries with, or "a pretext for putting oneself on display that virtually implies the deletion of all other concerns." Our best hope for bringing about a new way of looking at and constructing our art is to begin by constructing "a very different sort of integrating mythology." Gablik admits that with our present way of seeing the world, it's going to be difficult to envision art from a perspective of service or as something that isn't concerned primarily with itself.

### Art With an Integrated Perspective of Self and Landscape

What does art with an "integrated perspective" that includes both the self and the landscape look like? Is it even "art?" Isn't "art" by definition something we see inside galleries and museums? Sure, pre-historic people painted on cave walls and rock faces but we've come a long way since then.

The following examples show art created from a different perspective where the focus or desire isn't about having a show in a gallery, selling lots of paintings, making money and possibly achieving fame, but rather is about integrating itself inside an already existing landscape full of meaning, vibrancy and a communicative wisdom.

The first example of a different kind of art is that of Santa Fe artist Dominique Mazeaud and her art project *The Great Cleansing of the Rio Grande River*. Gablik calls Dominique's work an example of what a new relationship with art might look like and demonstrates what she calls "an integrating myth of compassion."

Dominique and I had become friends when I lived in Santa Fe some years before I read Gablik's book. I was happy to see an old friend of mine being singled out and celebrated for her artistry and sensitivity to connection with place. Years prior, when I had first heard about Dominique's art project from a mutual friend, I wanted to meet her and learn more about it. What could it mean to clean up a river and call it an art project? Was she retrieving interesting objects from the river and making re-cycled art from them?

As it turned out, when Dominique moved from New York to Santa Fe, she and I were both part of a spiritual group that met for spiritual ritual and sharing. When I asked Dominique about her project, she said that her inspiration to take care of the river had happened one day shortly before she left New York, when she was visiting in New Mexico and went for a walk with a Native American man along a stretch of the Rio Grande River in Taos. The riverbanks were littered with trash and it was in that instant, she says, that she knew something had to be done. And she knew that this "something" would be art-related. She envisioned it to be "a monthly performance whereby I would rid the river of trash, at one with so many others caring for rivers. I'd call it *The Great Cleansing of the Rio Grande.*"

For the next seven years, once each month Dominique walked the river in Santa Fe, with her large black plastic garbage bags and picked up trash from the river. She kept a journal of her experiences over those years and is now writing a book showing how she felt about the river, ritual, art and herself, which evolved over that time.

From her journal entry #7, she writes most poignantly:
*I feel for you, river*
*Bloodline of the Earth,*
*My mother....*
*Can I really imagine*
*That one day I could be*
*Living your suffering?*
*That I'd be forced*
*To ingest, like you,*
*The poisons*
*That are killing you...*

Later, she writes: "*During the early months, I tried to do some formal ritual introduction... But now, I have come to realize my heart's choosing is to be in the river, and* **picking up a can from the River,** *then another is itself a ceremony—contemporary ceremony.*"

As her journal entries progressed in time, she gradually transitioned into a deeper, more personal relationship with the river. In journal entry #11, she writes: *"Two more bags, so heavy I can hardly lift them off the ground. I don't count anymore. I no longer announce my 'art for the Earth' in the local papers. I don't report my finds nor my time for the newsletter* **Santa Fe Beautiful** *that had first supported my project by donating trash bags. Alone in the river, I make art by walking, bending, picking—simple gestures to sing my song of love."*

In journal entry #14, she begins to deepen her ideas about ritual. *"A ritual, in my book, should have as much inner depth as external action. What does it mean to cleanse the river? For the time it takes, I fill up plastic bags with whatever trash comes my way. That's what I do on the physical level. More and more, I understand it is what I bring to it that counts: my intention, vulnerability, and openness, my capacity to listen and share what I see, feel and learn; in a word, my love."*

Her beautiful and heart-felt entry from September 19, 1989, #25 asks: *"What is Art? What am I creating and whom do I serve? In the last few years I have lectured about* **Transformative Art: the Artist as Healer and Peacemaker**, *from NY University and Cooper Union School of Art to various cultural centers in Poland and Canada. I show the work of artists who have embarked on a different path than the ones who conform to the 'art for art's sake' tradition. In the post-modern era, definitions and expressions of art have stretched into new territories, recently hinting at* **art for life's sake**."

She continues in *The Great Cleansing of the Rio Grande River*, from her soon to be published book, *"By the time I was called to the river, my life had been woven of art. As a former gallery director working with established artists and then guiding younger ones, I was now called to join the ranks of artist myself. Entering this new territory, my response, whether felt inwardly or expressed out loud was* **"my heart is my medium."** *Artists are catalysts, whatever medium they choose. At the beginning, I did not miss a chance to plant a seed.*

*Religiously, I sent press releases to the local press and also wrote labels 'doing art for the Earth,' which I tied around the bags of trash. At first, I disposed of the trash myself with the help of a friend's pickup truck. Then one day I saw the City Sanitation truck come by while I was in the river—the labels must have worked! I climbed up to the bank then to the street where the truck was parked, and I thanked and treated him as a collaborator.*

*I kept my attention on doing. I felt so responsible that I talked of* **"putting in my day."** *Little by little, however, I relaxed my activist inclination and paid attention to the whole of me, to a deeper part of myself. To who I really was? To what was I trying to do? I stopped counting the bags. At one point, I even stopped being interested in what I perceived as the river's gifts.*

*Today I feel I was buying into the present system of art that is object-oriented. Is it because I am doing art for the earth that I need to produce something?*

*One Sunday, as I was performing the tasks of my Great Cleansing practice, picking up discarded cans people had thrown into the river and putting them in my bag as ritual receptivity, I happened to be near the Guadalupe Church when the bells rang out the hour. At that moment, I realized there was no difference between what I was doing in the river – loving/celebrating/honoring Her through my art-life* **heartist** *ritual – and what was happening inside the church in the name of religion.*

*Picking up a can*
*From the river*
*Then another*
*On and on*
*It's like a devotee*
*Doing countless rosaries*

*My getting acquainted with my river, all rivers, has stirred me into a new awareness. For all the years I have been frequenting my own river, on my way to one of the great rivers, the Rio Grande, I have deepened my understanding of life."* [4]

## The Snake Tree Art Project:

The second example of someone having a special relationship with the land and wanting to make an offering of an artistic kind is a personal one involving myself and a few other women living in Santa Fe a few years ago. The story of how this art project came about begins with a personal myth.

*Snake Peace Tree Project Participants*
Photo credit: Suzanne Canja

*Once upon a time a little girl was born whose mother dreamed of her birth long before she arrived. Night after night the mother dreamed of her daughter who would be born and always a snake would appear, as if to make the announcement of the little girl's birth. The mother was so concerned about the appearance of the snake in her dreams alongside her baby-to-be that she went to an old woman who lived on the outskirts of town to have her fortune read. The old woman read the tea leave remains in the bottom of the cup of tea she offered the concerned mother. "Not to worry," she said. "This daughter of yours will have a strong connection to all animals, not just snakes. She will be wise like the snake, have many friends and a good life. Go home now and start the preparations for she will be arriving soon."*

And, indeed, I did arrive soon on a cold, windy January day, a time when no one was about unless they had to be, much less a snake that hibernates in the winter. I would eventually learn that the snake is regarded by many cultures as a symbol for re-birth, wisdom and transformation, but it took me many years and deliberate efforts to learn about snakes beyond experiencing a frozen terror every time I saw one.

---

4    Dominique Mazeaud, *The Great Cleansing of the Rio Grande River*, from her soon to be published book.

Over time, with a great deal of concerted effort, I was able to call "snake" an ally. Like my mother, I had many dreams about snakes and knew I had achieved a new understanding of my relationship with snake when I had a dream of a large white snake that curled up and lay on my stomach while I slept. So in a certain way it was no surprise that one day while I was hiking near my home in Santa Fe, it occurred to me that certain sticks I saw laying on the ground, with their curves and different scaly surfaces, really looked very much like snakes. With no specific idea in mind, I began to collect a few here, a few there and brought them home, until one day I had accumulated quite a number of wooden stick-snakes.

These stick-snakes joined a very special "mother" stick-snake I'd found on one of my beach walks in Seattle where I'd lived until recently. The "mother" stick-snake was so artistic and powerful looking, with shells embedded all along its surface, surely a shaman's staff, and would serve as the guide and director of whatever was to come of this collection of other stick-snakes.

Suddenly, I got the idea to paint all my stick-snakes. As to what I would do with them once they were painted, I had no idea, but I knew I wanted to make an offering of some kind to the land to acknowledge how grateful I was to be back in the desert after living in the grey, drizzle of the northwest. One day I saw a post card showing an artist from the east coast who had hung numerous prayer flags from trees deep in the forest where they probably wouldn't be found or seen by anyone. Instantly, I knew that's what I wanted to do, create a "Snake Peace Tree" deep in the forest somewhere nearby and instead of brightly-colored flags, I would hang brightly-colored stick-snakes from the tree's limbs. It would be both an offering as well as a place for an unsuspecting hiker, if they looked closely enough, to see something a little unusual, perhaps giving them a moment of delight or opportunity to linger for awhile in peace and gratitude for the unexpected gift hidden in the forest.

After many hours of joyous labor collecting feathers, small stones, and assorted organic objects all of which would decompose over time, I began painting the stick-snakes and soon was joined by a small group of women friends for a "Snake-Painting Salon." First, I asked each person to write her own personal snake stories of their true experiences of snakes in a special snake journal I'd created. After accumulating a total of twenty stick-snakes, we headed out for the woods, carrying them in canvas bags and backpacks. We would hike deep into the woods to find the perfect trees for the Snake offerings we'd made to be hung.

What a glorious Sunday it was when the five of us plus beloved dog set out to one of the most beautiful and lush areas nearby with a waterfall and stream. Tall pine trees, aspen groves, oaks, the southwest cottonwood trees and juniper, as well as wild flowers greeted us on both sides of the trail and soon we were zigzagging back and forth across the river stream that rushed down from the Santa Fe ski basin. After choosing three perspective sights, we settled on one that had an enormous rock guardian that was planted in front of a grove of trees that hunkered over the beautiful mountain stream. It was a perfect place for the stick-snakes. After we smudged the beautifully decorated stick-snakes and made our statements of power and magic, we hung them on the tree branches. Afterwards as we lay peacefully and happily on a bed of pine needles, several hikers who passed by and saw the stick-snakes stopped to talk about the project. Most just said hello, smiled and walked on.

Part of my impetus for this art project came from the desire to be creative without the recognition of others to affirm that indeed I and the other women had created something called "art." I was inspired by the stories of ancient women of the islands of Malta and Crete who made beautiful objects and painted amazing wall murals but never signed their names. I was also inspired by stories of Native Americans, particularly the Hopi, who make offerings of their art to their families, villages or to their Kachinas, with not a thought of "this is mine and here's my signature, now acknowledge me."

I was most taken by a story I read in Jamake Highwater's book *Primal Mind* in which he says that it was considered a high honor to be given a song by a spirit or god, and that it was a special gift to you, one which you could sing to the sky or clouds or animals, maybe to the village, maybe not. The idea was that an individual did not own the song or creation; it was not theirs; it simply came through them. It was a gift from Great Spirit.

I wanted to experience how it would feel to invest quite a bit of my time creating something and then let it go, give it away, by placing it somewhere where no one might ever see it or if they did, wouldn't know who did this thing. No ownership...a Give-Away, and in this case, a give-away to the forest.

 WRITING EXERCISES

1. How do you think we should regard art in today's world? Can anyone be an artist? Do you think women are more in tune with an artistic process that includes a "relationship-based" art where they can see and appreciate the connectedness we all have with one another, including our connection to nature?

2. How might being in touch with your Wild Woman self assist you in feeling free enough to express yourself in anyway that pleases you? Does art have to have a "message" to be "good art?" What kinds of art do you imagine a woman of a wild nature might produce? What is your relationship with art and do you consider yourself an artist? Why or why not?

 ART EXERCISE

3. *WILD WOMEN MAKE ART.* Take any ideas you may have had from the art project stories told above or an idea of your own and envision an art project, ritual, painting, collage, decorated journal and so forth as your starting point. Select something that takes you outside your comfort zone of what you imagine you might be able to pull off! Ask a working artist or a friend who's artistic to help you with creating something that you may have seen in a dream, or in a painting, or on your last walk in nature. Keep a record of your process; i.e., what was the judging voice inside your head that kept saying you couldn't do this, or write about your fears, doubts and of course, your successes. Do you want to invite a few people to share in your completed pieces or projects? Maybe you want to create something in nature. Keep a record of all you experience, as that is a crucial part of the artistic creative process.

# Chapter 11: Wild Woman vs. the Borg

*Imagination is more important than knowledge.*
*For knowledge is limited to all we now know and understand,*
*while imagination embraces the entire world,*
*and all there ever will be to know and understand.*
~Albert Einstein

*A screenshot of the Star Trek: The Next Generation episode "I, Borg"*

Where are we today in our relationship with nature and technology? Are we rushing headlong into disaster and destruction created by our own hubris and lack of awareness and, some would say, lack of concern for any negative consequences resulting from our actions? When speaking about his clan's ancient prophecy foretelling how this world will turn out, one Hopi elder from the ancient tribe of Indians living in Arizona says we are in trouble. Known as Martin or Titus, he is a member of the Fire Clan, and keeper of the sacred tablet foretelling the future. Martin says the prophecy shows two possible paths for humans to take that will determine their future; one is the crooked path where humans no longer take care of each other or the earth, which will lead to destruction; the other path shows a future of harmony, balance and peace existing between people and the earth. Martin believes we have already chosen the crooked path.

The cacophony of doom is deafening. Environmentalists say we're past a tipping point because of the rapid species extinction and climate changes we're experiencing and hastening. Certain protestant religious groups point to the book of *Revelations* in the Bible's New Testament and say we are doomed and Armageddon is upon us. Sociologists and mythologist say we've lost our guiding stars of myth and sense of sacred place. Psychologists urge us to tend our souls while neo-shamans work to help us find them.

Super-smart killer robots rate pretty high on the list of doomsday scenarios that could wipe out the human race. In scientific circles, a growing number of artificial intelligence experts, including Stephen Hawking and Raymond Kurzweil agree that humans will eventually create an artificial intelligence that can think beyond our own human capacities. The moment in time when this happens is called the Singularity, which some say could lead to a utopia where robots would assume all the labor tasks once done by humans, allowing humans to relax and do nothing; or, it could lead to the A.I.'s killing off any creatures they see as competitors, for control of the Earth, such as humans. Stephen Hawking has long taken the view that the latter scenario is the most likely and could be the downfall of humanity. Raymond Kurzweil disagrees.

## Rise of the Machines: The New World Myth?

We are certainly at a critical juncture as we begin the 21st century regarding our relationship with spirit and flesh, or perhaps more accurately, body/nature and machine. A recent issue of *Wired* magazine featured the reality of a bionic human being in the next few decades. The technology of cyborgs and artificial intelligence beckons as a possible future for a marriage between humans and machines. What kind of *hierogamos* or sacred marriage would that be? And what would the offspring be from such an alliance, if it were possible? Can we take our hearts with us into what many would term, at best, an unholy alliance? Certainly machines promise a resiliency that humans, as carbon-based organisms made of easily destroyed flesh, don't have.

We are creating possible new futures all the time through our art, video and virtual reality games, stories, movies, music and science of what is and what might be, including the possible human, robotic entities and life on other worlds. What makes this particular time period so unique, and let's admit it, scary and exciting at the same time, is because the stakes are so high. We're talking about radical species extinctions and total devastating climate and global weather changes resulting in global mass human migrations. As animals and plants go extinct at an alarming rate, as global warming continues to rise and as earth changes continue to put greater numbers of human lives at risk, there is a palpable sense of urgency.

Is the Singularity near? Will the new story be how machines take over, as author and futurist Raymond Kurzweil says in his book *The Singularity Is Near* (2005)? Kurzweil predicts that's exactly what will happen. He says that by the end of 2020 computers will be capable of human-level intelligence; and by 2045 computers or artificial intelligence will exceed by about a billion times the sum of all the human intelligence that exists on the planet! At that point when computers surpass human intelligence, called the Singularity, Kurzweil says that this will result in, "a pace of change that will be so astonishingly quick we won't be able to keep up, unless we enhance our own intelligence by merging with the intelligent machines we are creating."

Kurzweil thinks that humans will be a hybrid of biological and non-biological intelligence that will become increasingly dominated by its non-biological component, but he maintains we have nothing to fear because "A.I. is not an intelligent invasion from Mars. These are *brain extenders* that we have created to expand our own mental reach. They are part of our civilization. They are part of who we are. So over the next few decades our human-machine civilization will become increasingly dominated by its non-biological component." In another book by Kurzweil, *The Transcendent Man*, he writes: "We humans are going to start linking with each other and become a meta-connection in which we will all be connected and all be omnipresent, plugged into this global network that is connected to billions of people and filled with data."

He recently said in a press conference that we are the only species that goes beyond our limitations, insisting that "we didn't stay in the caves, we didn't stay on the planet, and we're not going to stay with the limitations of our biology."

*Star Trek*, the well-known television series and movies have already explored the possibility of thousands of species being plugged into a global network, acting and thinking as one entity, which they called the *Borg*.

## But Can Our Technology Save Us?

A newly published book that describes how the earth will fare after global warming continues to rise has scientists and the public talking. Written by David Wallace Wells, *The Uninhabitable Earth: Life After Warming* tells us that the correct response right now should be one of fear and panic. In a chapter called "The Church of Technology" Wells dismisses the idea that our technology will save us, writing that we've used this refrain too often in the past, and all it has done is to allow us to simply carry on with our destructive habits without feeling too bad.

Wells reserves his harshest criticism for the tech giants and the accommodation by the American public of the moral corruption that he believes fuels Silicon Valley. "That technology might liberate us, collectively, from the strain of labor and material privation is a dream at least as old as John Maynard Keynes," he writes, and yet it is "never ultimately fulfilled." Instead, he says, we watch "rapid technological change transforming nearly every aspect of everyday life, and yet yielding little or no tangible improvement in any conventional measures of economic well-being."

## Does Connection Equal Isolation?

Sherry Turkle is a psychologist and cultural analyst at MIT who studies how our devices and online personas are redefining human connection and communication. In her most recent book *Alone Together: Why We Expect More from Technology and Less from Each Other*, she asks the reader to consider the question: "As we expect more from technology, do we expect less from each other?" Her answer is that we're letting technology take us places we don't want to go and should give more thought to the new kinds of connections we do want to have. In a recent TED talk, Turkle insisted that we're setting ourselves up for trouble in our communication with each other and with ourselves when our abilities for self-reflection are omitted. We're getting used to being connected *and* alone while seeking to achieve what she calls the "Goldilocks Effect," meaning we want to be not too close but not too far from those we're connecting with. When we post and text, she says, we can edit ourselves, present ourselves how we'd like to be seen whereas conversations and interactions that happen in real time with each other can't be edited or controlled.

Turkle says that one thing she hears all the time, especially among young people, is, "I'd rather text than talk." Another comment she often hears that troubles her, is, "I hope one day they'll develop a Siri on the I-phone that you can tell your troubles to because there's no one who has time to talk anymore."

She tells of a situation during a research study done in a home for the elderly that shows how we expect more from technology and less from each other. She describes seeing an elderly woman who'd recently lost her daughter who was pouring out her heart to a machine, called a sociable robot, because there was no one there, no human, who had time to listen to her.

Turkle thinks machines that offer companionship tempt us and, because of that, technology appeals to us where we're most vulnerable. She also thinks technology appeals to us because we're lonely but at the same time are afraid of intimacy.

From social media to sociable robots, she thinks we're creating an *illusion of companionship* without the demands of friendship. The illusion of never having to be alone that carrying around an I-Phone in our pockets gives us is central to changing our psyches, because the moment people are alone, she says, they become anxious or panic, start to fidget and immediately reach for a device.

Turkle believes that this constant connection is shaping an entirely new way of being that equates to: "I share; therefore I am." She thinks the problem is that we almost don't feel ourselves anymore so we reach out to connect more but in the process set ourselves up to be isolated. It becomes "connection equals isolation." For Turkle, this means a person doesn't develop the ability to be alone, or to value solitude. She writes, "solitude is where you find yourself and then you can reach out and form real attachments. The key is that if we don't teach our kids how to be alone, they will only know how to be lonely."

Some positive suggestions Turkle gives: Make friends with Solitude; create sacred spaces at home and reclaim them for live conversation; do the same at work; and listen to each other, including the boring parts. Technology is making a bid for how we connect with each other but Turkle remains optimistic and thinks that if we focus on how technology can lead us back to our own lives, bodies, communities, our politics and our planet, we'll be okay.

## The End or The Beginning?

So, are we looking at the end of the human race as we've always known it? Cultural historian William Irwin Thompson says in his book *Imaginary Landscapes* that we aren't looking at the end of the world but the end of a world system. He says that we are an emergent culture and the usual way a cultural shift happens is brought about through the death of the Establishment. According to Thompson, these emergent properties can be both unconscious and synchronous because there isn't one single and objective world we all live in. "The Princes of the church do not convert to becoming followers of Galileo; they simply die and a new generation comes along with a different historical orientation."[1]

Thompson explains this idea further in an essay called "The Borg or Borges" in which he says that whenever there is "a new emergent state of being in the transformations of culture, all of humanity does not immediately shift to the new mentality." He gives as an example an imaginary space voyager who wanders around Italy in the fifteenth century, interviewing people concerning their excitement at being alive during the Italian Renaissance. Thompson thinks that most of them wouldn't know what the interviewer was talking about because they were still living in the Middle Ages and would do so until their death. He says that the same is true now because most scientists and business people aren't aware of the implications of complex dynamical systems or of the cultural shift from modernity and the industrial nation-state to that of a planetary culture. At the end of his article, he gives a nod to Kurzweil when he

---

1    William Irwin Thompson, *Imaginary Landscapes*, p. III

says "With Ritalin in the schools, Prozac in the universities, Zoloft in the prisons, Ecstasy in the discos, and Viagra in the Senate, America can indeed be at peace with itself to let Kurzweil's machines inherit the Earth."[2]

 WRITING EXERCISES

1. The above material gives us a lot to unpack regarding our trek into the contemporary world where we live and make our home. Much of humanity is "wired" or connected through the Internet and other electronic devices. Some scientists see a more intensified connection with machines as not only inevitable but a great and marvelous advance for humanity while others are shocked and appalled at the prospect of melding into beings that are part human and part machine.

> Take some time alone in nature, perhaps leaning against a favorite tree or by a trickling mountain stream, and, using a stream of consciousness writing style, write your thoughts about what and where you see humanity going in the future. Include your fears as well as your imagination to make your own prediction of what might come to pass by writing a poem, story or drawing.

> How do you mesh living in the *now* with what might be considered a fearful prospect being proposed by science and many futurists as a point in time called the Singularity when machines will surpass humans in intelligence?

> Do you think we create or help to create our own destinies and if so, how do you regard our dance with technology and how we are raising our children?

> Write your response to the following statement: *The only enduring and possible new world that can come out of the chaos dynamic of current realities is one constructed by conscious nodes functioning throughout the entire web of connections, visualized by Hindus as the many-jeweled net of the Goddess Indra.*

> In your opinion, does much of technology and scientific thought omit the role that nature and the planet itself plays in our evolution of a possible future? Do you think embracing our wildness and keeping a strong connection with nature is more important than ever?

> What are the myths being constructed by science and technology's encompassing presence in our lives and what role are they playing in constructing our present and future worlds?

2. Think of Tina Turner's song "What's Love Got To Do, Got To Do With It?" Does love have any part to play in our present culture that is so technology-driven?

3. How important do you think it is that we stay informed and aware of what's going on in technology, regardless of our age?

4. Write a story in which the Wild Woman in the form of Artemis comes to visit our contemporary world. Choose a city as your setting and have her visit the local zoo.

---

2    William Irwin Thompson's essay "The Borg or Borges?" 2003, from his biography on www.Wikipedia.com

*Ceridwen's Cauldron of Inspiration*, from "Y Mabinogion" translated by J.M. Edwards (Wrexham, 1901).

# Chapter 12: Wild Women Take to the Land

*The sun shines not on us but in us. The rivers flow not past, but through us.*
*Thrilling, tingling, vibrating every fiber and cell of the substance of our bodies, making*
*them glide and sing. The trees wave and the flowers bloom in our bodies as well as our souls,*
*and every bird song, wind song, and tremendous storm song of the rocks in the heart of the*
*mountains is our song, our very own, and sings our love.*

~John Muir

*Maui Labyrinth*, Photo Credit: Suzanne Canja

According to Joseph Campbell, the sanctification of the local landscape is a fundamental function of mythology. The sense of the presence of creation, he says, is a basic mood of human beings, but because we now live in cities where "it's all just stone and rock, manufactured by human hands, making it a different kind of world to grow up in than when you're out in the forest with the little chipmunks and great owls. When you're out in nature, these things are around you as presences, and they represent forces and magical possibilities of life that are not yours, and yet, are all part of life and that open it out to you. Then you find it echoing in yourself, *because you are nature.*"[1]

For the poet and storyteller, mystic and seeker, wise ones and wild ones, both ancient and modern, the land with its beauty as well as ferocity is the source of creativity. Like the Wild Woman who seeks her origins inside an embodied earth, author and modern-day Druid Christine Worthington tells of her experience to reconnect with the land when she became part of the Order of Bards, Ovates and Druids. In an article "The Search for the Mabon,"[2] she writes about making a trip to Scotland after responding to a call from within urging her to reconnect with "a place whose heathered moors and mountain streams speak to my soul, a place where the spirits of the wind soar on eagles' wings in the high and wild places." She describes her experience of laying on the earth and letting the sun warm her body, and being aware that it was also warming her heart. Much as the Druids and bards who lived centuries before her

---

1    Joseph Campbell, *The Power of Myth*, p. 91
2    Christine Worthington, "The Search for the Mabon," p. 132, *The Druid Renaissance*
      by Philip Carr-Gomm

whose songs still echo across the landscape, Worthington speaks in poetic terms of her experience of the "deep and sacred knowledge" written in the earth itself, left there by ancestors in the stones, mounds, barrows and gateways. Like the Celts themselves whom William Butler Yeats declared "lived and died with the joyfulness of life," Worthington says that "the sacred and the sensual are united in the joy of being alive."

We are like the knight Percival, she observes, who goes in search of the Holy Grail but don't even know what questions to ask once he or we find it. There is a longing and a need to know how we can be of service in this life; a desire to connect with something deeper that unites the depths of our soul with the heart of the land we live upon. To her, the knowledge we seek is written *in star and stone*, something our ancestors knew. She writes that now is the time for us to listen once again to the wisdom of our ancestors to be found in the land.

Since the Celts were an oral culture, there is no actual body of recorded wisdom traditions. Much of what we know about them comes to us by way of Christian scribes who recorded their teachings and stories long after the demise of the Druidic orders, Pagans, or *Wicca*, witches. We do know that the Celts practiced an earth-based spiritual path and, according to author and contemporary Druid Philip Carr-Gomm, they viewed themselves as part of an animate, ensouled universe. According to the old stories, in the pagan Celtic wisdom tradition, poetry was regarded as a central skill for the seer and mystic. The poet and storyteller's relationship with nature was personal and intimate. Carr-Gomm calls it an authentic *I-Thou* relationship, going beyond our modern consciousness of *talking about* trees rather than *talking to* them. Interestingly, he tells of numerous poems written by people called the Wild Ones who lived a simple existence in the wilderness places.

These Wild Ones, often pagans, visionaries, hermits, or shaman were forest dwellers, living in huts made of wattles, or in caves or trees. Here is a poem showing the intimate relationship between one such wild one and the natural world:

> *Little antlered one, little belling one, melodious little bleater,*
> *Sweet I think the lowing that you make in the glen...*
> *Blackthorn, little thorny one, black little sloe-bush, watercress, little*
>  *Green-topped one, on the brink of the blackbird's well...*
> *Apple-tree, little apple-tree, violently everyone shakes you;*
>  *Rowan, little berried one, lovely is your bloom...*[3]

## Julia Butterfly Hill: A Contemporary Wild Woman

A modern day story that captures the intimate *I-Thou* relationship between ancient poets and nature as described by Philip Carr-Gomm is about a woman named Julia Butterfly Hill. When she was a young woman of twenty-five, Julia lived for 738 days between December 1997 and December 1999 in a 180 foot-tall, thousand year old California Redwood tree that she named Luna. Her intention was to

---

3 Kenneth Hurlstone Jackson. *A Celtic Miscellany*, as quoted in *The Druid Renaissance*, p. 287.

prevent the Pacific Lumber Company from cutting the tree down and to call attention to the devastation of the ancient forest. Similar to the ancient Celtic poets and storytellers referenced above called the Wild Ones, Julia took shelter in a small 6 x 8 ft. platform eighteen stories off the ground in the canopy of the tree she named Luna where she received supplies from the ground in a bucket tied to a rope.

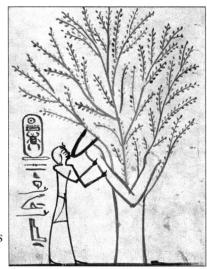

*Thutmosis III of Egypt:*
*The King Is Fed from the Holy Tree,*
circa 1500-1450 BC

Julia's story of how she ended up sitting in the top of a majestic redwood tree had begun a year earlier after she had been injured in a severe car accident, making it necessary to stay in the hospital for months. After she recovered, she sold her successful restaurant business and set out on a spiritual quest that eventually took her to Humboldt County, CA. where she joined with other environmentalists to protest the destruction of an ancient redwood forest. Initially, she volunteered to sit in the tree for thirty days but eventually decided to remain longer until Luna's safety was assured. Over the course of Julia's two years in the tree, she endured El Niño storms, helicopter harassment, a ten-day siege by lumber company security guards as well as the sorrow of seeing an old-growth forest's destruction.

After two years of her feet never touching the ground, Julia finally left the treetops of Luna when the lumber company agreed to preserve all the trees in a three-acre buffer zone; she had become a heroine, with many saying she was "the Rosa Parks of the environmental movement." She had never expected to receive all the honors that were given her after her experience of living in the tree Luna and has gone on to be an activist and spokesperson for the environment.

 WRITING EXERCISES

1.    It is easy to imagine that when Julia Butterfly-Hill, as she was eventually called, set out on a spiritual quest it was prompted in part by hearing and heeding the Call of the Wild Woman urging her to help out an endangered relative living in nature, the redwood trees. Julia tells of the strength and life lessons she gained from Luna in her book *The Legacy of Luna.*[4]

>    Have you heard the Call of the Wild Woman in your own life urging you to fight for our earth's legacy? Is there a particular animal, tree, forest, stream or mountain that resonates with you? If any of them are struggling to survive, what are you willing to do to make a difference?

---

4    See Julia Butterfly Hill's website: www.juliabutterflyhill.com to order the book on Luna and for more valuable information and inspiration.

2.  *The Legacy of Luna.* Today Luna stands tall on a ridge above the town of Stafford, CA and can be seen from Highway 101. Today, Sanctuary Forest, a non-profit land trust, tends to Luna's health after they negotiated a deed of covenant with the lumber company to serve as the tree's guardian. Luna stands as a beacon of hope reminding us of what individuals and communities can do to stand up for the rights of those who cannot speak, or, as we might say, those who speak but are no longer listened to except by the few.

> What are you willing to stand up for? Imagine yourself as a Wild Woman closely allied with nature. Write your heroine's story of taking a stand. Give us the setting, the details, what or whom you are attempting to help and what the final outcome is?

> On Julia's website, she says: "We are the ancestors of the future. What do you want your legacy to be?" Write your answer to this question.

## The Myth of the Celtic Goddess Ceridwen and Her Cauldron of Inspiration

In Celtic culture and mythology, female Goddesses dominated the mythical and literal landscape. The female deities, who represented the feminine principle of life, were seen as the embodiment of the Cauldron, the Grail and the Land itself. The goddess was personified throughout the living landscape, in its forests, rivers and hills. The contemporary Druid Philip Carr-Gomm says that in Ireland, for example, the entire country was once seen as a great goddess named Eriu, and her body was the land itself. In Country Kerry, there are two hills that to many resemble great breasts and are named the Paps of Anu, another of the goddesses' names. Trees, too, were seen as being ensouled, with each one having its own distinct qualities, such as the rowan's bright berries that gave protection from evil or the nuts of the hazel wood tree that bestowed wisdom. Animals were also seen as powerful allies and spiritual beings that could assist humans in connecting with the unseen realms or the Celtic Otherworld. Seers were known to foretell the future by watching the movements of birds and decoding their cries.

Like stories from other cultures of Goddesses and female deities, in Celtic lore the Goddess was both the giver of life and the destroyer. She took many forms revealing herself as the triple or three-fold deity, often appearing as a lovely maiden, kind mother or hideous hag. In the *Myth of the Cauldron of the Goddess Ceridwen,* she was seen as the keeper of a magical cauldron that contained the waters of inspiration, or *awen,* from which every bard or poet had to drink to be initiated into her secret mysteries. Celtic lore is replete with cauldron myths, many having to do with Ceridwen being a harvest goddess like Demeter, who provided the people with the food they needed to survive; but many other myths show her as the goddess of birth, death and transformation, as well as the giver of wisdom and inspiration for the creative arts of storytelling and poetry. Her cauldron not only contained the waters of inspiration but, after the first few sips, care was needed because its contents would become poisonous to the drinker.

Stories of Ceridwen as a giver of inspiration, of poetic and shamanic gifts are widespread, especially in poems ascribed to one of the Celts most famous bards, Taliesin. In a poem called *Hostile Confederacy*, Taliesin recounts the many mysterious transformations he has undergone through Ceridwen's cauldron, which has given him eternal life as well as wisdom. Here are a few lines from the lengthy poem that tell of some of his transformations:

> *"I have been a blue salmon,*
> *I have been a dog; I have been a stag,*
> *I have been a stump of a tree in a shovel; I have been an axe in the hand,*
> *I have been the pin of a pair of tongs; I have been a spotted cock,*
> *A hen became pregnant of me, With red claws and a cleft crest.*
> *I was necessitated to be nine nights in her womb as an infant....*
> *I have been a gift for a king,*
> *I have been dead. I have been alive.* [5]

Part of Celtic lore concerning the Cauldron of Wisdom says that nine priestesses were its guardians and "warmed it with their breath." The nine women who were the keepers of the sacred vessel were called the *Gallicenae* and remind us of the nine muses in Greek mythology who also gave inspiration, beauty and creativity to those who called on them. Resembling shamen or sorcerers, the *Gallicenae* were also said to possess the powers to raise winds and storms at seas; to turn themselves into animals and cure diseases incurable by others and, finally, were able to know and predict the future.

 WRITING EXERCISE

1. In keeping with the writing genre magical fantasy or magical realism, imagine that you are one of the nine women, the *Gallicenae*, who watched over the Cauldron of Wisdom. Set a story in the ancient forests or caves where seekers might have come to encounter the cauldron of wisdom and inspiration. Tell the story of someone who came seeking to drink from the Cauldron's contents and what the results were.

 ART EXERCISE

2. *CREATING YOUR OWN CAULDRON OF INSPIRATION.* Consider what Ceridwen's Cauldron of Inspiration is in your life. Using an actual object that resembles what this magical cauldron looks like to you, create your own Cauldron of Inspiration. Then, drawing on the story of Ceridwen, write a poem or prose piece telling of your own transformations after having drunk from Ceridwen's Cauldron.

---

5    John Matthews, *Taliesin: Shamanism and the Bardic Mysteries in Britain and Ireland, pp. 318-319.*

MORE WRITING EXERCISES

3.    Imagine the landscape where you live as being the actual body of a great female being. Can you identify certain features in the landscape that resemble her face, her body, or other physical attributes? What would you name the streams, mountains, or forests? Set a story, either in past or present-day time, inside this newly envisioned and animated landscape. Describe the people you find there and what they are doing and saying; What concerns them? Do any of them resemble your own family or what you might consider your "tribe?"

 ART EXERCISE

4.    *MASK-MAKING.* Imagine a communion with wild animals and birds, where the boundary between human and wild animal is blurred. This is the province of the great seers who "walked between the worlds." It is also home of the archetype of the Wild Woman.

>    Begin by collecting items to make a mask for your Wild Woman persona; feathers, yarn, paints, and other special items to attach to either a ready-made mask, or one you will make from strips of *Plaster of Paris.* Before you begin your mask-making project, spend time reflecting on the material above and identify any animal that has special significance to you. Perhaps you are drawn to the wolf, or cougar; eagle or raven; snake or dolphin. This project is best done with a partner, especially if you choose to hand-make your mask with plaster strips.

>    Once you have completed your mask, create a special ceremony to be performed in the woods, near an ocean or mountain stream, or an isolated desert place. Then write about your experience in your journal. Be sure and hang your mask in a special place to continue your communion with the spirit of the wild animal that originally spoke to you and represents your connection with your Wild Woman archetype.

 MORE WRITING EXERCISES

5.    John Muir was a Scottish-born American naturalist and early activist for the preservation of wilderness. Sometimes known as "John of the Mountains," one of his many famous quotes was "Think Like a Mountain." As I have thought about John Muir's statement over the years that we should "Think Like a Mountain," I have come to see it more as "Be the Mountain." Write your ideas of what those two statements mean to you. Then, write about any experiences you've had with a mountain, tree, river or rock that has reconnected you to the land in such a way that you felt no separation.

6.  Japanese mountaineer Junko Tabei was the first female to climb Mt. Everest in 1975, defying stereotypes in a country that saw woman's place as in the home. She founded the Ladies Climbing Club in 1969 with the slogan "Let's go on an overseas expedition by ourselves," and as the leader of the climbing party of an all-female Japanese team, together they scaled Mt. Everest. Later in her life, she had become concerned about the degradation of Mt. Everest and all the garbage that was being left on the mountain. She was quoted as saying "Everest has become too crowded. It needs a rest now." She kept climbing even after being diagnosed with cancer four years before her death in 2016.

    > What qualities or archetypes do you think Junko Tabei possessed that enabled her to step outside the cultural norms for women of her time and place? Write about a time when you or someone you know stepped outside the norms of what was expected of them and accomplished something astounding.

    > Do you see any difference in people who go into wilderness places for recreation or to challenge themselves physically than someone who goes there to experience the solitude or a sense of the sacredness embedded in nature?

7.  Read the following *Declaration of Commitment to the Earth, Our Communities, and Ourselves.* Then write a declaration of commitment of your own that tells how you feel about taking back the land and keeping it safe for all that live there.

    *We declare and know that we are priestesses, healers, wise women, and shamen with responsibilities to heal our communities, our sacred mother earth and ourselves. Although linear time and space separate us from our ancestors, we claim the sure knowledge of all our relations: past, present and future, to provide us with the wisdom to once again walk with great intention and harmony upon the face of the earth.*

    *We commit ourselves to once again remembering the ways of our ancestors who walked with beauty and awareness upon the earth. We call upon our ancestors to guide us in this undertaking to learn and study their old ways so that we might carry the dream forward, so that we might fill our bodies with light drawn from the re-telling of the old stories which inspired and united our ancient kin to walk a spirit-filled life while sojourning on earth. We trust and affirm that we are drawn to this study by the power of our inner knowing and by the wisdom of our ancestors. We commit to this undertaking and intend that it bless our families, our community, and the world.*

*Taos Pueblo: Inhabited For Over 1,000 Years.*
Photo credit: Marjorie St. Clair

# Chapter 13: Call of the Wild Woman

*It may be that some little root of the sacred tree still lives.*
*Nourish it then, that it may leaf and bloom and fill with singing birds.*
~Black Elk, Sioux Medicine Man

In the previous chapters we have focused on myths, archetypes, and stories with an intention of letting them guide us towards a re-discovery and reconciliation with the archetype of the Wild Woman and our wildish instinctual natures; seeking to let them guide us to a greater and fuller understanding of what we stand to lose if we don't recognize that we are part of an amazing network of living beings, and that we must use all our resources and talent to protect the earth, which is our home. In addition, through various writing and art exercises we have immersed ourselves into the deepest layers of our psyches where we confronted our own unredeemed aspects of sloughed off ugliness, rage, despair, and bitterness; where we found and re-connected again with our often famished instinctual Wild Woman self; where we realized how much we need her help to stay rooted in nature and to reconnect with our larger purpose of being self-aware human beings who are compassionate, responsible and loving.

By examining a variety of myths and stories from numerous cultures and sources, we have opened our eyes; we have listened and heard the *Call of the Wild Woman* and her Song of the Earth celebrating the gifts and beauty of nature. We know that now is the time to re-create our own personal as well as collective myths and stories that reflect the new place we inhabit in the world narrative, one that instructs us to respect the collective wisdom of our ancestors and the embodied wisdom of the Earth itself and beyond, to include the story of the Universe.

## Earth's Song: Verse One: Seeking Beauty

Joseph Campbell, author and foremost mythology scholar, said that presently there are two kinds of myth: personal and societal. There's the mythology that relates you to your nature and to the natural world that you're part of, and another mythology that is strictly sociological and links you to a particular society or group. In myths that exist in a particular sociological community, aggression is projected outward. He gives as an example the Ten Commandments from the Bible that says, "Thou shalt not kill," but then in the next chapter says, "Go into Canaan and kill everybody you find there." Campbell called this a "bounded field" in which myths of participation and love only pertain to the *in-group* to which a person belongs and the *out-group* is regarded as totally other. He considered the biblical tradition to be a socially oriented mythology, one in which nature was condemned; and because of this view, humans felt they had to control it or try to control nature, which gave rise to tension and anxiety, and ultimately, according to Campbell, saw the decimation of the natural world and the annihilation of native peoples.

Campbell said that the sociological function of myth has taken over the world and is out of date. He says that the biblical story we have in the West was based on a view of the universe belonging to the first millennium B.C. and didn't accord with our present understanding of either the universe or the dignity of humankind. The biblical myth belongs entirely to another time, he said, and we have to learn how to align again with the wisdom of nature and realize our alliance with the non-human inhabitants.

Primal cultures of the past and present times consider the world to be alive, animated and to evolve as a living organism. Many people today call this idea *pantheism,* because it suggests that a personal god is supposed to inhabit the world, but Campbell said that definition was misleading and didn't correctly convey the idea at all. He considered the idea of *pantheism* as being *trans-theological* because it describes an un-definable, inconceivable mystery or power that is the source and supporting ground of all life and being.[1]

Campbell believed that individuals had to find an aspect of myth that relates to their own life, and could serve a pedagogical function, instructing them how to live as a human being under any circumstances. He wrote that the only relevant mythology for today would be a mythology of the planet, which he believed didn't exist. The closest thing he saw to a planetary mythology he believed was to be found in Buddhism that sees all beings as Buddha beings. But the problem, to his thinking, was that people haven't come to that recognition or awareness.

## Women, the New Cultural Mythmakers

Do women have a special role in creating the new cultural myths or even a planetary myth that we need to *dream the dream forward,* to use Carl Jung's phrase? While living in Santa Fe some years ago my interest in the relationship between women and mythology peaked as I began to observe more closely the role I saw women playing in maintaining and creating an expansive mythic culture out of which their imaginations regarding the future could take hold, root and grow. Since Santa Fe was percolating with amazing, creative women who were contributing to the community in countless ways, I imagined a television series to highlight some of them and their ideas about the importance of mythology in their lives, culture and the planet itself. I decided to call the series, "Women, the New Cultural Mythmakers," and began to contact women whose "difference was making a difference" to use author and professor Mary Catherine Bateson's phrase based on her idea of life as being an improvisational art form. I proposed my idea for the series to the administrator at the public access television station run by Santa Fe Community College, who gave me the go-ahead and the six-part series was born.

---

1    Joseph Campbell, *The Power of Myth*, p. 31.

Preparation of the material I wanted to explore with the women guests during the series' hour-long segments was an extension of my ongoing inquiry and theory that women were, in fact, playing a major defining role in shaping and creating a path for the future born out of their personal experiences and understandings; and that women were living lives that provided the necessary substantive material for the new narratives they were giving birth to.

*Storyteller Under Sunny Skies* by Rose Pecos-SunRhodes, Jemez Pueblo, NM, The Children's Museum of Indianapolis, *Creative Commons Attribution-Share Alike 3.0 Unported license.*

I was deeply influenced by Mary Catherine Bateson's book *Composing a Life* in which she said that women needed to reinvent themselves again and again in response to a changing environment and proposed a *model of improvisation* as providing a more creative and appropriate approach to life than the model of a single-track ambition. Bateson, daughter of two famous parents, anthropologist Margaret Meade and cyberneticist Gregory Bateson, said she found herself looking at the patchwork of both her personal and professional achievements and questioning how they fit together and whether or not they composed or even began to compose a life. In this questioning process she decided that the place to look for the key to discovering *new patterns* was to be found in women's lives because they were clearly composite. She felt that such a key might be helpful in understanding how women could make sense of what was often *interrupted and discontinuous lives.*

A *composite life*, Bateson suggested, posed the recurring riddle: what do the parts have in common? This riddle, in turn, led her to ask a series of other riddle-like questions to discover what the parts had in common with the whole: "How is a lady like a soldier? Why is caring for an infant like designing a computer program? How is the study of ancient poetry like the design of universities?" She followed up these questions with this advice to women, *"If your opinions and commitments appear to change from year to year or decade to decade, what are the more abstract underlying convictions that have held steady, that might never have become visible without the surface variation?"* [2]

As I looked for women to be part of the first show *Women, the New Cultural Mythmakers* whom I felt represented Bateson's *model of an improvisational life*, I invited three women: stand-up poet and teacher Judyth Hill, recipient of the Witter Bynner poetry grant to write and create poetry performances with Santa Fe teenagers; Lena Bartula, artist and owner/director of Guadalupe Fine Art a contemporary art gallery on Canyon Road; Director of Exhibitions for the annual celebration of the Virgin of Guadalupe and board member of the Santa Fe Council for the Arts; and Katya Miller, jewelry designer of cultural, historical and spiritual amulets, and other ritual objects; part of the Alameda Co-Housing Community and videographer for the NM Jewish Historical Society.

Once everyone arrived in the television studio and had been fitted with a microphone, the studio director signaled the okay and the cameras began to roll, I smiled and began the interview by introducing the bold idea that women and their role in culture was that of mythmakers, a role they expressed through art making and other creative endeavors, which ultimately re-shaped it and them in the process. The purpose of the series, I said, was to explore the multiple processes of mythmaking in current use by women and to discern the direction these processes were taking them and their

2    Mary Catherin Bateson, *Composing a Life*, p. 15.

communities. I continued by saying that in the past, new myths often arose in times of profound cultural crises and great change, such as existed in our current society. I called attention to two present-day major shifts happening for women for the first time in history: large numbers of us were free to pursue activities of our own choosing outside the home; and secondly, many women no longer regarded procreation as their primary role in life. Such profound changes and shifts in a woman's personal and political situation would likely affect our cultural values and be reflected in our stories and mythology. The logical place, then, to look for such new and long-term effects was in the creative works and lives of women.

*Baby Swallows,*
Photo Credit: Marjorie St. Clair

The answer to what women are saying through their art, ritual, poetry and other modes of creative expression, I said, was evident in each of the three guests, who in her own right was part of that growing group of creative individuals playing a significant role in creating the myths and stories defining our current and future culture.

Poet Judyth Hill made the observation that myths allow us to drop down to a deep place where we can share more of who we are, giving us opportunities to explore where we are all humanly "one." In women's art and poetry, she said, the issues were about freedom, with a lot of emphasis being on images of a Goddess.

Reading from her book *Goddess Café*, she recited a poem "Women and Death" in which she says women are comfortable with death and are being re-born through their bodies.

Lena Bartula, art gallery owner, said she was seeing the emergence and creation of altars and shrines of all kinds dedicated to Tara, Earth Mother, and the Virgin of Guadalupe, all of which connect us from the personal level to the universal. She talked about her ongoing *Shrine Project* begun in the 1990s that focused on creations by women and were displayed around Santa Fe.

"These shrines heralded a week long celebration of the Virgin of Guadalupe in which artists and galleries observed the Guadalupe's feast day, beginning on December 12th, she said. "In Santa Fe you can see the Guadalupe as the one who connects the tri-cultures of whites, browns and indigenous; the artists with the writers; the Catholics with the Jews; because She has no borders, no boundaries. She's part of Santa Fe. She's like the Good Mother/Bad Mother syndrome, however, because life in Santa Fe can be tough as well as nurturing."

Katya Miller, jeweler and community activist, said she was learning how to pause and be alone in order to be able to create, a pause that afterwards enabled her to come to a place where she wanted to communicate with others. She viewed community based art projects and rituals as a way to recognize the sacred that's all around us, and that gives us ways to re-spirit what's already there. She gave as examples the three large sculptures situated in front of the Santa Fe Capital; a sculpture called *The Earth Mother* by a woman sculptor from Jemez Pueblo; another sculpture *Women Water Carriers* that stands next to a third sculpture *Maiden-Mother-Crone* created by local and internationally acclaimed sculptor Glenda Goodacre. "With a group of other women, we recently did a ritual of prayer to strengthen the feminine principle and to honor water as an important source of all life," Katya said. She also mentioned several other statues that represented the feminine; one in particular called "Freedom" that is located on top of the Capital building in Washington, DC. "She goes unseen," Katya said, "but the more we tune into her, however, the more we can tune into the deep spirit of the country because she blends the two cultures, the Native American and European. She wears an eagle headdress, embodying the Iroquois Indians and the European because she's dressed in European clothing."

All three women thought that myths focusing on women claiming their equal place in society and stories of the goddess or a divine feminine were conduits for healing of self and the larger culture from which they emerged and were embedded. They all agreed that we are creating the new consciousness through our collected stories when we women evolve our archetypes and re-vision our relationship with the Earth.

 WRITING EXERCISES

1. Do you think women have a particular role in creating the new cultural myths that will sustain, nourish and help humanity survive and move forward in positive ways?

2. Take a moment to consider the personal and professional achievements in your life. Do you feel that they come together to form a composite life? Do you think your life more accurately fits Bateson's *model of an improvisational life*?

3. What do you think about Joseph Campbell's idea that the only relevant mythology for today would be a mythology of the planet? How important do you think a new myth that aligns with the wisdom of nature is?

The New Feminine Mysteries

Taking certain wisdom ways and ritualized traditions from our ancestors that honored the Earth and cared for all life is a place to start in evolving our new stories that help us learn to live in harmony and respect for all of creation. Looking to the archetypes of Athena and Ariadne who were both weavers, we can begin by weaving aspects of the ancient wisdom of our ancestors with the emerging consciousness of the sacred feminine into what we writers like to call, a narrative story arc. This new story we are telling in the 21st century has already been building and growing into a collective myth for some time now; eventually, it will become a story broad and deep enough in scope, meaning and content to include everyone in the human and non-human family. It will be a myth or a series of myths that show how we can evolve by learning compassion for all existence. It will be, in essence, the New Feminine Mysteries in which the feminine principal is once again restored to its proper place of honor alongside every other aspect of the living universe.

First, we must begin by re-learning how to deeply love the physical world again and our bodies... our Wild Woman self.

Secondly, we must take responsibility for our home, planet earth and all its inhabitants. This can be as simple or complex as we can imagine and commit to accomplishing. The Hawaiians have several words that explain this concept: *Ho'ee*, which means, "Respect, one for the other;" and the second is a phrase, *malama the aina,* or love the land. If you love the land, it will take care of you.

Thirdly, performing personal or group rituals to re-animate and re-connect to the spirit of place, to each other and to nature are important. Taking positive actions on your own or in a group to educate regarding the environment and/or for holding our politicians and legal system accountable, these are some of the many ways to re-affirm the sacred in everything.

 ART EXERCISE

1. *Seven Arrows* is a book by Native American Plains Indian Hyemeyohsts Storm that describes his culture and a wisdom path called the *Medicine Wheel.* Storm's book documents the destruction and demise of his people by re-telling the stories through which much of their wisdom was taught. In Storm's book he speaks of the wisdom traditions and symbols belonging to various medicine (healing) Shields that were created by the people to identify themselves. In particular, he describes one shield called *Shield of the Four Stars* that represented the four daughters of Mother Earth and the four directions. He describes the four women on the Shield of the Four Stars as follows:

   The Northern Star on the Shield is the *Woman of the North* who covers the earth with her colors
   of winter. She freezes everything and makes the colors dance with her ice crystals. She is
   Wisdom and her color is white.

   The Southern Star is the *Woman of the South*, or the Gift Sister. The South is a time when the
   waters run freely and the whole world becomes green. It is the time of innocence, trust and
   the Give-Away. Her color is green.

   The *Woman of the East* is the golden haired star woman and her colors dance bright with her
   beauty. *The Woman of the East* touches the Day with her morning light and welcomes new
   beginnings. Her color is yellow.

   The *Woman of the West* spreads her colors and unites them in her evening sky. The *Woman of the
   West* touches the Night and knows the darkness. Her color is black.

   The *Shield of the Four Stars* shows the four sisters, all daughters of Mother Earth. In the center of
   the shield is a Great Painted Lodge, the place where all four women originated.

   CREATE YOUR PERSONAL STAR WOMEN SHIELD. A personal shield was intended to let others know who you were, whose clan you belonged to and what your spirit allies that guarded or protected you were. The shield might be carried in an individual's medicine bundle or rolled up and carried with the person when they traveled.

Creating your own *Personal Star Women Shield* is a way to choose how you want to identify yourself. It provides you with a visual way to tell your own individual, personal myth. Spend some time reflecting and writing about the Four Stars or Women you want to symbolize on your personal shield. You might want to draw your *Personal Star Women Shield* on a piece of beautiful paper and hang it somewhere that you can see; or, you may want to make an actual shield using an animal skin or piece of material that you can draw on.

 WRITING EXERCISES

2.  *YOUR ANCESTORS.* By remembering your ancestors and reconnecting with your own cultural traditions, you reconnect with that which animates your soul and the group soul into which you were born. Many of us today are being called to remember our native ancestry roots, as well as our mythic heritage that often has very limiting religious traditions in order to heal what has been transmitted to us that is broken and in need of replacing with new stories, new ways of sharing our collective wisdom and new ways to live co-creatively and with compassion for others.

    > Spend some time researching your ancestral tree for yourself and your family from the many online sources; and/or talk with family members as to what they remember about your great or great-great-grandmothers and grandfathers, aunts and uncles. What were the religious or spiritual roots and beliefs of your ancestors? Did any of those beliefs or traditions inform your growing up years and do they play any part in your present day life? In what ways did any "religious" traditions or myths negatively impact you? Do you consider yourself to be on a spiritual rather than religious path?

3.  The history of life on earth has seen one people-tribe-country after another invading or being invaded and destroying the other's entire way of life. There is an obvious pattern of repetition in this re-occurring annihilation of "other." Much of this conflict has been born out of conflicting religious mythologies.

    Joseph Campbell had some very instructive things to say about what he called "religious mythologies and metaphor" and how they have shaped our world and humanity. "If you have a mythology" he said, "in which the metaphor for the mystery is the father, you are going to have a different set of signals from what you would have if the metaphor for the wisdom and mystery of the world were the mother. And they are two perfectly good metaphors. *Neither one is a fact.* They are metaphors. It is as though the universe were my father. It is as though the universe were my mother. Jesus says, 'No one gets to the father but by me.' The father that he was talking about was the biblical father. It might be that you can get to the father only by way of Jesus. On the other hand, suppose you are going by way of the mother. There you might prefer Kali, and the hymns to the goddess, and so forth.

That is simply another way to get to the mystery of your life. You must understand that each religion is a kind of software that has its own set of signals and that will work." [3]

Campbell went on to say that the three great religions, Judaism, Christianity and Islam all have three different names for the same biblical god, yet they can't get along with each other. They're stuck with their metaphor and don't realize it's just a reference. Each group says, "we are the chosen group and we have God." According to Campbell, everything is already there in their myths that say love *thine enemy* but because theirs is a closed circle, what he called a "bounded field" community, it doesn't allow for anything but a literal interpretation. He says that the only way to keep an old tradition going is by renewing it in terms of our current circumstances.

> What is our role here and now, as part of a vast ecosystem that we are hastening to its demise with our own reckless and shortsighted behavior? Can mythmaking or storytelling make any difference?

> Write your ideas in response to what Campbell had to say about the three great religions and "religious mythologies and metaphors."

---

3   Joseph Campbell, *The Power of Myth*, p. 20.

# Chapter 14: Where the Wild Things Are: A New Story

*This is what is the matter with us, we are **bleeding at the roots,***
*because we are cut off from the earth and sun and stars, and love is a grinning*
*mockery because, poor blossom, we plucked it from its stem on the tree of Life,*
*and expected it to keep on blooming in our civilized vase on the table.*
~D. H. Lawrence

The planet Earth herself is the source of a new paradigm for expanded vision and spiritual evolution. Her story is our story. That the Earth is a conscious, evolving entity was known and acknowledged by the ancient goddess-worshipping peoples as well as many native traditions of today. For example, the Navahos call the Earth Mother "Changing Woman" because she changes aspects with the seasons. The Taos Indians of New Mexico honor the Earth and her cycles by calling all activities to a halt on their pueblo from early December to January because they believe Mother Earth is sleeping under her blanket of snow and all must walk softly so as not to disturb her; to them, this is the period of time between the Earth's death and rebirth and is to be observed as a time for staying still.

*Planet Earth as Seen*
*from the Apollo Spacecraft*

## Coming Home: Embodied Wisdom from the Earth

Scientist James Lovelock's *Gaia Hypothesis* also describes planet earth as a living, evolving organism, with her own intelligence structure to be honored and acknowledged. Lovelock's point of view holds that the "light body" of the planet which is embedded in the planet's memory program, which he calls a "Psi Bank" or global brain, is activated by the conscious, cooperative effort and vision of everyone and everything that lives, moves and has its being on the earth's body. In short, everything we do affects everything else. We are all connected. If we pollute the earth, then we pollute ourselves.

If we reflect on the planet as a living being as many scientists and others do, we might wonder, "is the Universe itself a living, creative entity?" In the old deterministic paradigm of Newtonian science, Isaac Newton described the universe as a vast machine, which eventually gave rise to a mechanistic worldview and became the dominant metaphor for how people and organizations function and live together in the world. Its mantra was "measure and quantify" and meant that truth could be observed, weighed and measured. However, in the living world of much of today's science, scientific investigation has uncovered that living forms in many seemingly mysterious ways, combine the stability of structure with the fluidity of change. Like the example of whirlpools, living systems depend on a constant flow of energy through them; like flames, they transform the materials on which they feed to maintain their activities and to grow; but unlike whirlpools or flames, living structures also develop, reproduce and evolve. In the late 1930's Austrian biologist Ludwig von Bertalanffy called such living structures "open systems" to emphasize their dependence on continual flows of energy and resources from their environment to stay alive. He maintained that living systems are open systems that operate far from equilibrium and possess self-regulation processes.

Certainly, this shift in perception from ecosystems to the planet as a whole, or to a global network of processes of production and transformation, informed the work of James Lovelock in his *Gaia hypothesis*.

## A Confluence of Sound and Story: A Musical Narrative

For many people who take a holistic approach to life, there is a Divinity that is immanent in nature and the world. So, how does the Creator deliver its creations? Some fascinating ideas worth considering come from a scientist named Rupert Sheldrake. Sheldrake earned his PhD in biochemistry from Cambridge where he was director of studies in cell biology for a number of years. In his book *The Presence of the Past* he presents his interesting and unusual ideas about how nature and the cosmos works. His central notion is an idea he calls *morphic resonance*, which he describes as being "like the known fields of physics and are non-material regions of influence extending in space and continuing in time." Basically his book explores the possibility that memory is inherent in nature and that each natural system which can be as diverse as those of termite colonies, pigeons, orchid plants or insulin molecules, inherit a collective memory from all previous things of their kind, no matter how far away they were or however long ago they existed. An example of this collective memory can be seen in male humpback whales that every year sing a new verse to the song they were singing the prior year, taking up where they left off. Sheldrake says that such habits may be inherent in the nature of all living organisms, in the nature of crystals, molecules and atoms, throughout the entire cosmos. He ultimately sees the entire cosmos as one evolving organism.

Sheldrake's *morphic resonant fields* gives credence to the idea that everything is part of a sound harmonic, some sort of resonant field that is operating or existing within a Cosmic Symphony that plays its never-ending Cosmic Song of Creation. Are we not all a confluence of sounds, a musical narrative if you will, each a part of and reflection of the Cosmic Song of Creation? Sharps and flats, dissonant as well as harmonious chords and sounds; rhythms, obscure and familiar; instruments of infinite shape, texture and variety, playing out the ever-changing and never-ending song that not only shaped humanity and the earth but the entire cosmos? We can never comprehend it all, of course, just as we could never comprehend all that exists in our own imaginations, or Sheldrake's *morphic resonant fields*, much less comprehend all that exists in the Creator's Imagination.

In his well-remembered interviews with Bill Moyers for the PBS series on mythology Joseph Campbell said that we needed to change our myths; that we needed a larger story, one that didn't divide us along the lines of "our story is THE story; our god is THE one and only god: our truth is THE truth." In fact, he said, we need a planetary story.

Presently, or so I am imagining, the collective human story unfolding on Planet Earth seems rather unimaginatively and continually stuck at the part where the *Dark Forces of Violence and War-Mongering* fight the *Light Forces of Peace and Good Will.* In order for the collective story to move forward, something's gotta give. Imagine you were forever playing any majestic symphony that kept repeating the middle movement or a single movement.

*The Path Forward*
Photo Credit: Suzanne Canja

Some repetition helps establish a theme, of course, and gives continuity; however, at some point, a resolution begs to be heard. Having said that, however, not all musical compositions or stories have a linear structure, preceding from an Act I, the set-up, to Act II, the conflict, to Act III, the resolution. Maureen Murdock in her book *The Heroine's Journey* sets forth a different storytelling model that she says grows out of a woman's experience that resembles a spiral structure rather than a linear one. Then there are primal cultures, such as the Hopi Indians of the southwestern United States who have no past or future tense in their language, resulting in all stories happening in the present tense, the now. Believe me, this can be very confusing. On one particular visit to see my Hopi friend who lives on the reservation, she kept talking about her sister coming by the house. Later, I asked the person who had brought me about this, "I thought Freida's sister was dead; so why does Frieda keep saying she's coming by this afternoon?" To which he replied, "her sister is dead." "But I don't understand," I protested, thoroughly confused until he explained that there is no verb tense but the present in the Hopi language.

Or, take the model for storytelling from the Aboriginal people of Australia who say that their stories originate from the land itself and that the people learn them when they do their "walk-about" and live in the Dream Time.

Perhaps we poets, storytellers and narrators of a New World Myth must look for a new storytelling template, one that moves the story of humanity and Planet Earth past the War and Peace segment, which is what mythologist Joseph Campbell insisted we must do. I remember a young man's perfectly amazing comment that he didn't want to go to heaven when he died because it would be totally boring, "just a bunch of Angels singing and playing harps all day and who would want that?" he asked, a notion I rejected but secretly had to admit that the way he put it did make heaven sound a bit boring or at least monotonous, which leads back to my original comment that stories, musical or otherwise, that repeat themselves over and over can become unimaginative and maybe even destructive. As educators have learned about gifted children, and what child is not gifted in their own special way, they easily become bored or wish they could be playing video games when either the material to be learned is irrelevant or is presented in a manner that stimulates *repetitious feedback* instead of creative engagement.

This example from education can also be applied to the greater collective of humanity; i.e., many of us are just plain exhausted and split open with grief at the repetitious War and Peace narrative that never moves to any kind of creative resolution, or more to the point, we just want a new story altogether. War and Peace is a very popular storyline, however, one that has literally been repeated for thousands of years.

Apparently, there just hasn't been enough interest, or conscious awareness, to sustain and move off the old narrative or storyline to a new plot or a new template. Perhaps "heaven" for those of us who are intent on creating a new narrative for peaceful co-existence and mutual creativity, is a state of "higher" consciousness, higher in the sense that peaceful states of mind and peaceful actions arise from and vibrate at a higher sound resonancy, and, if this *morphic resonant field* notion is correct, it extends to some kind of cosmic consciousness. Obviously this "heavenly" state of conscious awareness creating itself over and over again like a fractal or fractured landscape, or a hologram, or a dream inside an ever-changing and beautiful repetitive cosmic imagination, requires no belief in a "savior" or a dying-resurrecting god figure, as noted above in Campbell's comments. As Campbell so convincingly noted in his hundreds of hours of recorded interviews on mythology with Bill Moyers, these old storylines no longer serve us in the twentieth-first century.

## Earth's Song: Verse Two: *Les Chansons des Roses*

*Garden Rose*
Photo Credit: Marjorie St. Clair

I'm an avid gardener and take a personal interest in all my plants, noticing the ones that are thriving and those that are droopy and need some extra attention. I often talk to the surrounding plants that are doing well and encourage them to help their droopy neighbors. One particular summer morning when the entire garden was flourishing, I heard a *Chansons des Roses*, or Songs of the Roses. The numerous blooming roses were singing a chorus so vibrant and joyful, they seemed to be shouting,, "All is Beauty! See the Beauty! All creation lifts up its voice in celebration of life! Here we are! We are alive!" Needless to say, I was pretty blissed out.

Later, when I came inside and was still in a state of awe at hearing the songs of the roses, I listened to some of my favorite contemporary music by Ola Gjeilik called *Northern Lights* and performed by the Phoenix chorale. I was brought to tears and spent all morning reflecting on the Beauty that music brings and how Nature is the source of all the singing and song making by humans and every other living creature that participates in the Earth's Song. Will we ever understand what's going on in this earthly and cosmic drama? I wonder. Probably not, but I think we touch on its meaning with our music; with our stories and songs of poetic verse, painting with color and sculpting with clay; with selfless acts of kindness; when we laugh; during quiet moments of deep reflection and thankfulness; when we touch bodies with another in tenderness and passion; when we are filled with compassion and joy for Earth's human and non-human beings. As in romantic poet John Keats' words: "Beauty is truth, truth beauty. That's all you know on earth and all you need to know."

Every day presents an opportunity to live in beauty, walk, talk and breathe in beauty. In a world full of violence and devastation, with leaders whose bellies are full of undigested acts of greed and whose speech is incomprehensible and toxic, seeking beauty in the ash heaps of the world's inhumanity to others and in graveyards of the tortured dead where once ancient Yoginis gathered to do rituals of re-generation, seeking beauty is an act of power and boldness; a story like no other.

How best then to strike the ever elusive balance in all things? How to immerse ourselves in the soothing bubble bath of Trust? How to remember to listen to the song of Nature constantly throbbing with sound, holding together the whole visible universe and beyond in its web of sound? In listening to the *Call of the Wild Woman* and following her lead, we may yet find a way through this perilous journey to stay human. We need not continue to "bleed at the roots."

## In Heaven and On Earth: A New Template For Storytelling

"In Heaven and On Earth" has always been a potent part of humanity's collective story. We look up into the starry heavens with awe, as our original ancestors must have done hundreds of thousands of years ago. From the beginning, so the stories of primal people tell us, humans looked up and declared, "we are from the stars and when we die, we shall return." It was as though our sojourn on Planet Earth was but one of many that we as star people were destined to experience along our infinite journey through the Cosmic Universe.

Perhaps this larger perspective of a journey through an evolving cosmos with no time limitations or place restrictions is a template large enough to contain the infinite stories imaginative, creative storytellers will tell, all reflections and fractals of an Ultimate Creator Being inside a holographic universe.

 WRITING EXERCISES

I.  Why do we make stories? Why do we ask "why am I here?" Why is that question and the pursuit of its answer so all-consuming? Asking "why am I here?" is really several other questions: "Where did I come from?" and "Is there more to life than what's in front of my eyes?" In our effort to answer these questions, we made up stories of creation, gods, monsters, and super heroes and how it all works, with the more subtle explanations leading to the unknowable, or as some call it, the Great Mystery.

Jesuit Priest and paleontologist Pierre Teilhard de Chardin who died in 1955 had his own planetary vision for humanity, which he called the *noosphere*. He defined the *noosphere* as a new unity rooted in love and based on knowledge, which he believed was the next phase of human evolution.

> Take some time to create a new narrative that explains how we arrived at the place we currently occupy on planet Earth. Include in your story arc a *different, imaginative resolution* to the Earth's Story. (A reminder from information in earlier chapters that not all cultures, presently or in the past, see life on planet Earth in terms of dualities.)

2. Barring miracles, how might we think about the transition to a world that is peaceful, just and sustainable? If, two hundred years from now, we have achieved such a world, what industrial illusions and technological fantasies were jettisoned along the way? Do you think our stories can restore in us a balanced and peaceful way to live?

3. Barbara McClintock won a Nobel Prize for the discovery of gene transposition in corn plants and the way she did her research was by *listening to the corn.* This was a great shock to the scientific community when it found out about how she did her research, which she described as intimately getting to know each plant of corn and the "story" as she called it, of each plant. She found what the other members of the scientific community wanted to know but weren't able to discover through their learned methodologies.

> If the ability to see and the ability to listen are not valued; if the ability to make connections and to live relationally are not valued, what does this culture value? Can new stories in which we come together and consciously create a collective narrative bring us to a new place where we are once again embedded inside the collective memory, or dream of the Earth? Write what you imagine is the Dream or Song of the Earth, in which the Earth is the main character and narrator of the storyline.

4. Imagine you are going to give a TED talk on a new narrative for Planet Earth and the future. Write your talk and give it to a group of friends or arrange to do an actual TED presentation. This is your story, your narrative of how to dream the dream forward and deserves to be heard in whatever way you decide.

# Bibliography

Abram, David. *The Spell of the Sensuous*, NY: Vintage Books, 1997.

Baring, Anne & Jules Cashford. *The Myth of the Goddess: Evolution of an Image*, London: Penguin Books, 1993.

Barnes, Craig. *In Search of the Lost Feminine: Decoding the Myths That Radically Reshaped Civilization*, Colorado: Fulcrum Publishing, 2006.

Bateson, Mary Catherine. *Composing A Life*, NY: Penguin Books, 1990.

Berry, Thomas. *Creative Energy: Bearing Witness for the Earth*, San Francisco: Sierra Club Books, 1988.

Boissiere, Robert. *Po Pai Mo: The Search for White Buffalo Woman*, Santa Fe, NM: Sunstone Press, 1983.

Bolen, Jean Shinoda. *Goddesses in Everywoman: A New Psychology of Women*. San Francisco: Harper & Row, 1984.

*Goddesses In Older Women: Archetypes in Women Over Fifty*, San Francisco: Harper, 2001.

*Crones Don't Whine*, Boston: Conari Press, 2003.

Campbell, Joseph. *The Power of Myth*, New York: Doubleday, 1988.

*The Hero's Journey*, San Francisco: Harper & Row, 1990.

Carr-Gomm, Philip. Editor. *The Druid Renaissance*, London: Thorsons, 1996.

Chatwin, Bruce. *The Songlines*, NY: Penguin, 1987.

Daly, Mary. *Beyond God the Father*, Boston: Beacon Press, 1985.

Downing, Christine. Editor. *The Long Journey Home: Re-visioning the Myth of Demeter and Persephone for Our Time*, Boston: Shambhala, 1994.

Drysdale, Vera. *The Gift of the Sacred Pipe*, Norman: Univ. of Oklahoma Press, 1982.

Eliade, Mircea. *Cosmos and History: The Myth of the Eternal Return*, NY: Harper, The Bollingen Library, 1954.

Feuerstein, Georg. *Sacred Sexuality: The Erotic Spirit in the World's Great Religions*, Vermont: Inner Traditions, 1992.

**Gablik, Suzi.** *The Re-enchantment of Art,* NY: Thames & Hudson, 1992.

**Gimbutas, Marija.** *Goddesses and Gods of Old Europe,* Berkeley: University of California Press, 1982.

   *The Language of the Goddess,* San Francisco: Harper & Row, 1989.

**Glubok, Shirley.** Editor. *Discovering the Royal Tombs at Ur,* Toronto: The Macmillan Company, 1969.

**Graves, Robert.** *The White Goddess: A Historical Grammar of Poetic Myth,* NY: Vintage Books, 1959.

   *Adam's Rib & Other Anomalous Elements In the Hebrew Creation Myth,* NY: Thomas Yoseloff, 1955.

**Hall, Calvin.** *A Primer of Jungian Psychology,* NY: New American Library, 1973.

**Hall, Nor.** *The Moon and the Virgin,* NY: Harper & Row, 1980.

**Harding, Esther.** *Women's Mysteries: Ancient & Modern,* NY: Harper, 1971.

**Hays, H. R.** *The Dangerous Sex: the Myth of Feminine Evil,* NY: Pocket Books, 1954.

**Herrera, Hayden.** *Frida Kahlo: The Paintings,* NY: Harper Collins, 1991.

**Highwater, Jamake.** *Myth and Sexuality,* NY: Penguin, 1990.

**Hill, Julia Butterfly.** *The Legacy of Luna,* NY: Harper Collins, 2000.

**Kane, Herb.** *Pele: Goddess of Hawaii's Volcanoes,* Copyright 1987 by Herb Kane.

**Kurzweil, Raymond.** *The Singularity Is Near: When Humans Transcend Biology,* NY: Penguin, 2005.

**Lady Gregory.** *Irish Myths & Legends,* Philadelphia, Running Press, 1998.

**Lind, L. R.** Editor. *Ten Greek Plays,* Boston: Riverside Press, 1957.

**Lippard, Lucy.** *Overlay: Contemporary Art & The Art of Prehistory,* NY: The New York Press, 1983.

**Luke, Helen.** *The Perennial Feminine,* Parabola, Vol. V. No. 4, NY: 1980.

**Matthews, Caitlin & John.** *Ladies of the Lake,* London: The Aquarian Press, 1992.

**Matthews, John.** *Taliesin: Shamanism & the Bardic Mysteries in Britain & Ireland,* London: The Aquarian Press, 1991.

**Murdock, Maureen.** *The Heroine's Journey: Woman's Quest for Wholeness,* Boston: Shambhala, 1990.

**Neumann, Erich.** *Amor and Psyche: The Psychic Development of the Feminine.* Bollingen Series 54. Princeton: Princeton University Press, 1955.

   *The Great Mother: An Analysis of the Archetype.* Bollingen Series 47. Princeton: Princeton University Press, 1955.

**Pagels, Elaine.** *The Gnostic Gospels,* NY: Vintage Books, 1981.

**Perera, Sylvia.** *Descent to the Goddess: A Way of Initiation for Women,* Toronto: Inner City Books, 1981.

**Pinkola Estes, Clarissa.** *Women Who Run With the Wolves: Myths & Stories of the Wild Woman Archetype,* NY: Ballantine Books, 1992.

**Qualls-Corbett, Nancy.** *The Sacred Prostitute: Eternal Aspect of the Feminine,* Toronto: Inner City Books, 1988.

**Sheldrake, Rupert.** *The Presence of the Past,* NY: Vintage Books, 1989.

**Shaw, Miranda.** *Passionate Enlightenment: Women in Tantric Buddhism,* Princeton, New Jersey: Princeton University Press, 1994.

**Spretnak, Charlene.** *Lost Goddesses of Early Greece: A Collection of Pre-Hellenic Myths,* Berkeley: Beacon Press, 1992.

**Stone, Merlin.** *When God Was A Woman,* Originally published in Great Britain under title *The Paradise Papers* by Virago Limited, 1976.

**Storm, Hyemeyohsts.** *Seven Arrows,* NY: Ballantine Books, 1972.

**Thompson, William Irwin.** *Imaginary Landscape: Making Worlds of Myth and Science,* NY: St. Martin's Press, 1989.

   *The Time Falling Bodies Take to Light: Mythology, Sexuality & the Origins of Culture,* NY: St. Martin's Press, 1981.

**Von Franz, Marie Louise.** *The Feminine In Fairy Tales,* Boston: Shambhala, 1993.

**Wallis, Velma.** *Two Old Women,* NY: Harper Collins, 1993.

**Wittig, Monique.** *The Guerilleres,* London: Pan Books, 1972.

**Wolkstein, Diane & Samuel Kramer.** *Inanna: Queen of Heaven And Earth,* NY: Harper & Row, 1983.

**Woodman, Marion.** *The Pregnant Virgin: A Process of Psychological Transformation,* Toronto: Inner City Books, 1985.

CPSIA information can be obtained
at www.ICGtesting.com
Printed in the USA
LVHW060348291220
675317LV00026B/346